Rehabilitating Blind and Visually Impaired People

Rehabilitating Blind and Visually Impaired People

A psychological approach

Allan Dodds

Deputy Director
Blind Mobility Research Unit
Nottingham

CHAPMAN & HALL

London · Glasgow · New York · Tokyo · Melbourne · Madras

Published by Chapman & Hall, 2–6 Boundary Row, London SE1 8HN

Chapman & Hall, 2-6 Boundary Row, London SE1 8HN, UK

Blackie Academic & Professional, Wester Cleddens Road, Bishopbriggs, Glasgow G64 2NZ, UK

Chapman & Hall Inc. 29 West 35th Street, New York NY10001, USA

Chapman & Hall Japan, Thomson Publishing Japan, Hirakawacho Nemoto Building, 6F, 1–7–11 Hirakawa-cho, Chiyoda-ku, Tokyo 102, Japan

Chapman & Hall Australia, Thomas Nelson Australia, 102 Dodds Street, South Melbourne, Victoria 3205, Australia

Chapman & Hall India, R. Seshadri, 32 Second Main Road, CIT East, Madras 600 035, India

Distributed in the USA and Canada by Singular Publishing Group Inc., 4284 41st Street, San Diego, California 92105

First edition 1993

© 1993 Chapman & Hall

Typeset in 10/12 Palatino by Mews Photosetting, Beckenham, Kent
Printed in Great Britain by St Edmundsbury Press, Bury St Edmunds, Suffolk

ISBN 0 412 46970 7   1 56593 153 X (USA)

A catalogue record for this book is available from the British Library

Library of Congress Cataloging-in-Publication data

Dodds, Allan.
    Rehabilitating blind and visually impaired people : a psychological approach / Allan Dodds. – 1st ed.
        p. cm.
    Includes bibliographical references and index.
    ISBN 0-412-46970-7 (acid-free paper)
    1. Blind–Orientation and mobility. 2. Blind–Psychology.
3. Blind–Rehabilitation. 4. Visually handicapped–Psychology.
5. Visually handicapped–Rehabilitation. I. Title.
HV1598.D63 1993
362.4′18′019–dc20   93-16158
                                                        CIP

∞ Printed on permanent acid-free text paper, manufactured in accordance with the proposed ANSI/NISO Z 39.48-199X and ANSI Z 39.48-1984

This book is dedicated to
Hugh Farquharson

Contents

Preface

The precursor of this book, entitled *Mobility Training for Visually Handicapped People*, received a most favourable response from reviewers and readers alike. It was felt that the aim to present psychological material to non-psychologists had been largely successful, and that the relevance of the material to professional practice had been made clear. However, many people expressed a wish that the book had been longer and had included more details of practice than had been possible in the brief space available. Some readers said that they had found many of the ideas raised to be fascinating in themselves, but dealt with too cursorily to be intellectually satisfying or practically useful.

Also, with the creation of the new role of Rehabilitation Worker in the United Kingdom, there is a need to include material relevant not only to mobility, but to independent living in general, although the fundamental principles are still best understood in the context of the visual control of movement. However, it has to be recognized that in countries other than Great Britain, orientation and mobility are still the province of one professional worker, so that the text places a greater emphasis on mobility than on other independent living skills.

One must also acknowledge that although research has been carried out for over two decades into various aspects of blind mobility, correspondingly little or no research has been carried out on the acquisition of independent living skills such as those of communication and daily living. As a consequence of this, there is no specific body of knowledge of how these skills are best taught or what factors are involved in their acquisition. Indeed, as independent living skills utilize a wide variety of very different devices ranging from the trivially simple to the most sophisticated that technology can devise, there can be no general account of the acquisition of skills which may be so diverse as to defy classification.

However, the author is keenly aware that there exist well-established principles by means of which any task whatsoever may be understood, and readers are urged to consider adopting the task analysis approach suggested and illustrated in the text, using their imagination in applying the general principles outlined to specific areas of task acquisition. The general, psychological factors addressed throughout, however, apply equally to independent living skills where new behaviours have to be acquired at a time when the individual may be least ready to display competence.

A further inclusion of material relates to the need to expand upon the effects of brain damage on perception, thinking, feeling and behaviour. Many clients have suffered strokes or head injury with its associated brain damage, and they present with their own special combination of deficits, some of which they may be largely unaware of. Without a proper assessment of residual function much time can be wasted and unnecessary frustrations experienced, to the detriment of the relationship between client and specialist. Therefore another aim of this edition is to maintain sight of the integrity of the person in the face of loss of function and to deal with the individual at a personal level.

I have resisted the temptation to write a chapter on clients with a dual sensory impairment. There are two reasons for this. The first is that I have had little first hand experience with this special, very heterogeneous group. The second is that an entire book could be devoted to the topic, and no-one to my knowledge has yet written one. Rather than plagiarise existing material to form a separate chapter, I have directed the reader to such relevant material as exists. However, the general psychological principles outlined are as applicable to clients with a dual sensory impairment as they are to those with only one.

It must also be recognized that people generally live their lives in the company of other people with whom they share their daily hopes and fears. Any attempt to restore a person's independence without the recognition that your attempts may produce the need for change in other members of the family is likely to be less than optimally successful. Only by involving the family as a whole in sharing or negotiating their aspirations for your client as well as his own can you hope to ensure a successful outcome for everyone concerned.

Finally, I have become acutely aware of the fact that most professional workers with visually impaired and blind people are working under considerable amounts of stress. This is due to a variety of factors, but with foreknowledge, the worst effects of stress can be avoided and when it does manifest itself steps can be taken to reduce it. Therefore the final chapter of the book includes an account of what has come to be known as 'burn-out', an only too common occurrence in the helping professions and one to which the most enthusiastic and committed workers are the most prone.

In order to escape the criticism of using sexist terminology, I have elected to refer to the rehabilitation worker as 'she' and the client as 'he' throughout, rather than to use the clumsy 'he/she' construction. In cases drawn from real life, the gender of the client is maintained, but anonymity is ensured by the use of a pseudonym. I have also used lower case for various occupational titles, except when it is important to distinguish between the generic term 'rehabilitation worker' and the specific title of Rehabilitation Worker. It is hoped that the reader will find these conventions acceptable.

Those, then, are the aims of this book. It is hoped that, by the inclusion of this additional material, a more comprehensive account of the acquisition of independence skills will have been presented to the reader and that the rehabilitation worker will find herself in an even stronger position to deliver the specific skills of mobility and independent living to clients experiencing a wide range of difficulties of which their visual impairment may only be one. It is also hoped that the various training bodies will think fit to use the text at least as an accompaniment to, if not part of, the core of existing training courses which may not have

easy access to the psychological material gathered together
here.

Allan Dodds
Blind Mobility Research Unit
University of Nottingham

Acknowledgements

It would not have been possible to gather together all the material presented in this book were it not for two important factors. In the first place, the Department of Health has funded the Blind Mobility Research Unit at Nottingham for a number of years now, and over these years I have had the opportunity of meeting countless blind and visually impaired people, together with those involved in their rehabilitation. The work has taken me all over the United Kingdom, and I have also been fortunate enough to be able to attend international conferences where I have had the opportunity of meeting fellow academics as well as practitioners. Second, I have been privileged to work in a university department which has provided a constant intellectual stimulus to my thinking. In particular, I wish to acknowledge my indebtedness to Professor Ian Howarth, founder and current Director of the Blind Mobility Research Unit, my mentor in my early years, and constant support in my later ones. Without giving me the freedom to follow my nose in such a rich field of enquiry, the material gathered together here might have remained scattered in many disparate sources and as a consequence been unavailable to many workers.

A number of individuals deserve special mention for their conscious as well as unwitting contributions. David Lee of the University of Edinburgh gave me the unique perspective on perception which has enabled me to make sense of blind mobility in particular and the non-visual control of movement in general. Diana Seybold of the Australian Association for the Blind gave me the confidence to adopt the broad framework presented in Chapter 1, and to deliver the punches where they might be felt in Chapter 11. Pat Fleming of Nottingham-shire's Visual Impairment Team allowed me to pick her brains on several occasions. Dinah Northall, Science Librarian, saved my bacon by her splendid detective work. An anonymous reviewer of an earlier draft of the manuscript provided a number of very helpful suggestions which have improved the book, and graciously pointed out the odd schoolboy howler. Last, but not least, my wife and family gave me the space to work inside my mental bubble for many months. To all of those people, and countless more, too numerous to mention, who have helped me in so many different ways over the years, I give my unreserved thanks.

The preparation of illustrations has been greatly helped by a number of individuals and organizations. I wish to acknowledge my gratitude to the City of Birmingham Museum and Art Gallery for allowing me to reproduce Figure 1.1 in Chapter 1; to Eleanor Gibson for permission to reproduce Figures 4.1 and 4.2 in Chapter 4; to Tony Heyes for producing Figure 4.6; to Nurion Industries Inc. for permission to reproduce Figures 4.7 and 4.9, in Chapter 4, and to Methuen & Co. for permission to reproduce Figures 5.1, 5.2, 5.4 and 5.5 in Chapter 5. I also wish to express my gratitude for the technical assistance received from the Psychology Department at the University of Nottingham. I would like to thank Howard Wilkinson, Head of Technical Services; Hazel Flannigan, and Lisa Ng for their help in preparing Figure 8.1 in Chapter 8 and for proof-reading the manuscript; Carl Espin for his friendship over the years, and Steve Tristram for assisting in the production of many of the illustrations. Special thanks go to Catherine Walker of Chapman & Hall for her help and encouragement during the sub-editing stage. Any errors remain the responsibility of the author.

1

Blindness: implications of the term

Sudden and severe loss of sight can be an overwhelmingly distressing experience for the sufferer and, equally, those close at hand. This is particularly true when the individual has enjoyed normal or near normal vision for most of their life and as a result has taken their sight completely for granted. Although, a slow, progressive deterioration in sight can be compensated for to a large extent by minor adjustments to expectations and behaviour, there eventually comes a point at which the individual realizes that their visual impairment is severely handicapping them in daily activities such as shopping, cooking, feeding, dressing, house-work and mobility; not to mention leisure activities and hobbies through which they might otherwise obtain some respite from the irritations of visual impairment. It is when there is little pleasure left in life and nothing other than the repeated experience of frustration that the person is likely to come into contact with one or other of the helping professions, possibly for the first time in their lives.

Although visual impairment is recognized at the legal level in terms of the labels 'blind' or 'partially sighted', such labels are largely unhelpful when trying to understand what effects the visual impairment is having upon a person's lifestyle, and on the lifestyles of those around them. The degree of severity, its rapidity of onset and the nature of the impairment are all likely to determine how the person responds to the situation. Most registered blind people will have some degree of residual vision, but between 5% and 10% of them will be virtually unable to make out anything more than changes in light levels, such is the degree to which their eyes or their visual systems have been affected. An even smaller percentage will be totally unable to perceive even bright sunshine. These totally blind people are the exception rather than the rule, and they may rightly resent being referred to as 'visually impaired', 'vision impaired' or 'visually handicapped'. However, the majority of registered blind people will benefit from not being referred to as blind.

In some ways, the totally blind client presents fewer problems to the rehabilitation worker in terms of skill acquisition than does the person with residual vision. This is true for at least two reasons. First, there is no need to assess residual visual functioning in order to decide how to proceed: one simply teaches alternative methods which have been worked out satisfactorily years ago. Second, the training under sleepshade that one has had oneself makes it easy to understand the totally blind individual's difficulties from the inside and to have complete confidence, born out of first-hand experience, that the standard solutions work. When dealing with a client with residual sight one has less confidence in what one does because how the world appears to them is largely unknown and, as we shall see, assessing residual vision comprehensively is a laborious, time-consuming and often difficult task.

On the other hand, the client who has suffered a sudden and severe loss of sight is not in the same position as a sighted person who has just donned a sleepshade for the purposes of understanding that it is possible to deal effectively with the environment without the benefit of sight. The trainee worker has the luxury of being able to take off their sleepshade and escape into the reassuring world of the sighted where simple tasks can be carried out automatically and without the need for careful planning. One can relax in the knowledge that should any sudden demand present itself, then it can be dealt with swiftly and effectively without any real stress being experienced.

The blind client does not have this escape route and they are firmly stuck with their blindness for the rest of their lives. Some clients cannot bear to face this fact and decide there and then that life is not worth living. They will either retreat into a world of passivity and self-pity from which they may never emerge, or they may even initially panic and try to take their own lives. At the time when you visit them with an offer of rehabilitation they may well have made their minds up that rehabilitation may work for other people, but that in their case, since nothing can be done to restore their sight, then nothing can ease their pain. Part of your job may be to persuade them that life without sight is not the living death which they may imagine it to be, before you even begin to give them the independence skills which will later prove your point.

However, although acquiring independence skills will help a totally blind person to adjust to their new status at a behavioural level, many further adjustments are needed on the cognitive and emotional levels. For some people, total loss of sight deprives them of the familiar visual feedback that reminds them of who they are. We may shudder when we see our reflections in the mirror first thing in the morning, but at least we are reminded of our existence in a way which is denied a totally blind person. Going suddenly blind, therefore, can threaten one's identity to such an extent that the individual may well feel that they are going mad, or losing their grip on reality. John Hull, the author of a remarkable book on how he fought against the experience of total blindness (Hull, 1990), mentions time and time again of his struggle to maintain contact with people and with the outside world, and his book should be obligatory reading for those who have worked for so long with blind and visually impaired people that they may have long forgotten what the experience of total blindness is like.

Some people, on losing their sight, may undergo a severe personal identity crisis, and this may cause them to begin to question aspects of themselves as fundamental as their gender. I have personally come across men who have chosen to adopt a female role once they have lost their sight, and who wish to be recognized as women when they present for rehabilitation. Whether such behaviour is evidence of previous gender identity problems which blindness offers a means of exploring, or whether the traditional masculine role is no longer as easily accessible as the traditional female one, is more a matter of conjecture than anything else. However, I do suspect that the deep and equally intense emotions unleashed by sight loss can bring some men face to face with aspects of themselves which they have hitherto regarded as feminine, and which they may wish to develop, perceiving that the more macho side of themselves can no longer be easily expressed. In all cases of threatened identity, counselling and psychotherapy offer the appropriate atmosphere in which these deeply personal issues may be discussed, reflected upon and where some sort of sense can be made of the confusion.

REGISTRATION

The act of registration may be considered to be what sociologists and anthropologists call a *rite de passage*. A rite de passage is a social marker that one's role in life has changed, such as marriage or divorce, or 'coming out'. Registration as a visually impaired person means being officially labelled as a person who belongs to a minority group identifiable in that its members are somehow different from 'normal', i.e. the majority of people. It requires considerable courage to face the fact, and huge emotional and practical resources to grow into that new role. Registration means 'going public', and partially sighted people in particular may prefer not going public because there are few obvious benefits which accrue to them and plenty of negative expectations which accompany the process.

A recent survey carried out by the Royal National Institute for the Blind (Bruce, McKennel and Walker, 1991) found that there was a large number of eligible, but unregistered people around, and that as a consequence of not being registered they were less aware of services than those who were registered. Registration can therefore be seen to serve as a trigger to receiving rehabilitation services, and the view that it only serves to stereotype must be balanced against this realization. Perhaps social services staff need to recognize both the importance of registration and its consequences and implications, spelling out to the client why it is better to be placed on the register and emphasizing the positive aspects of it.

STEREOTYPING, STIGMA AND CHARITY

It was Helen Keller (the bane of most blind people in that she had to excel at everything she did) who recognized that blindness itself was not the primary handicap, rather the attitudes of sighted people towards 'the blind'. The term 'the blind' is used for effect. Notice how it places a barrier between our ability to empathize with another human being who may just happen to be unable to see, but who is otherwise embedded in the same human condition as ourselves. Keller realized this, and yet, over one hundred years after her birth people still like to think of 'the blind'. Why should this tendency to objectify and pigeon-hole people be so seductive?

Victorians, in their own inimitable way, managed to deal with the contradictions between their world view and their behaviour by means of institutionalized hypocrisy, much of which we have inherited. Industrial capitalists exploited the ordinary person, treated women and children as chattel, polluted the environment and generally helped the wretchedness of humanity along quite a considerable way. Unable or unwilling to stop these practices, they chose instead to salve their consciences by doing good works on an individual basis; setting up charitable institutions on a collective one, and selecting individuals or groups of individuals as worthy recipients of what they assuredly believed was one of their finer emotional virtues, namely pity.

This sentimentality is still alive and well and with us today. The major charities for blind people in the United Kingdom still refer to 'the blind' in their titles, thereby helping to perpetuate the myth that people registered blind cannot see at all. Advertisements are placed in the press and on public hoardings which terrify people into believing that being registered blind means being unable to see even daylight, and that this suddenly happens to 40 people each day in Britain. By means of these advertisements, sighted people are manipulated to feel pity for those less fortunate than themselves, or even guilty that they are better off than them. This formula produces what I like to refer to as the PTL syndrome (no, not Praise the Lord; rather, Produce the Loot) which charities need to do in order to survive. But the effect of subscribing to such illusions is that the negative stereotype of the poor blind person who must feel forever grateful for any scrap of charity is perpetuated down the ages, and a role in society is created which newly registered blind people can readily take upon themselves.

The perniciousness of this world view should not be underestimated. If society embraces negative stereotypes of blindness then it is little wonder that when a sighted person loses enough of their sight to be eligible for registration as a blind person they should readily cloak themselves in a mantle of negative stereotypes purveyed by their own culture. For what other images of blind people do they have other than those available in society? Few sighted people have ever met a blind person, so that positive role models in the form of competent and independent blind people are largely unavailable to them. All that most people have to go on are images of blindness perpetrated by the media; the visual arts, literature and drama. As we shall see, these are far from encouraging; tending to stigmatize, rather than to offer positive aspirations to those who themselves might one day lose their sight (Lee and Loverage, 1987).

The term 'charity' literally means 'love', but it has unfortunately become associated with emotions such as virtue and pity, so that those who work full-time for charities accrue a high status in the eyes of the world. They experience emotions such as pride in their choice to do good works rather than to make lots of money, perhaps at the expense of other people. Yet those who work for charities out of the very best of motives often slip imperceptibly into a sense of self-satisfaction bordering on self-righteousness or even smugness. They can lose touch with the predicament of those whom the charity is designed to help. The higher the person rises within the organization, the greater is the temptation, and the perks to be had cannot be underestimated. As Brandon (1988) reminds us, life looks different from the inside of a BMW.

IMAGES OF BLINDNESS

Images of blindness in the visual arts abound, dating back to antiquity. The depiction of blindness in art is usually made for one of two reasons. It either makes some moral point or other, or it invites the viewer to have a particular emotional response to the predicament of the blind person. Paintings of Christ restoring the blind man's sight, of which there are many, produce the emotional response they do because they feed upon an unconscious attitude which regards blindness as the worst of all possible human afflictions. Since Christ is supposed to represent the greatest symbol of love, the

Figure 1.1 *The Blind Girl,* by Sir John Everett Millais.

greatness of his love is revealed when he removes the greatest of afflictions. A picture of Christ miraculously removing a hang nail would hardly have the same impact, because hang nails are perceived as being just a nuisance, and there are less dramatic ways of dealing with them.

Sir John Everett Millais' painting *The Blind Girl* evokes in the viewer a mixture of feelings, but there is a preponderance of negative ones as far as one's attitudes towards blind people are concerned (Figure 1.1). The central figure, a young blind girl, is seated by a stream in a meadow bathed by the brilliant light of a sun which has just come out after a passing rainstorm. Her right hand lightly grasps a blade of grass; her left clutches the hand of her companion, perhaps her sister, who leans against her as she witnesses the rare sight of a double rainbow in the sky behind her. She is dressed in russet brown which matches her vivid, auburn hair, and her skirt is patched and torn. Unknown to her, a red admiral butterfly has alighted on her shawl, and on her knee rests an accordion. Around her neck a notice reads 'Pity the blind'.

The girl's clothes tell us two things: that she is poor, but that they have been chosen by someone who obviously cares about her appearance. But although the colours are an extension of her own, she herself has no way of appreciating this. Nor is there any way in which she can see, hear or feel the gaudy butterfly which sits on her shawl. Her main contact with the world is through her sister's hand and eyes, and she relies on her sister's description of a scene to which she has no direct access. To the uninformed viewer, her only experience is that of touching the blade of grass, and her experience of anything beyond that is vicarious.

The effect of these perceptions on the viewer is to produce an overwhelming feeling of sadness in the face of the visual beauty with which the artist confronts us, but which is forever denied the girl. The exhortation to pity her is not simply social comment; it goes further in that it anticipates the effect of the picture on the sensitive viewer, or tells the viewer how to feel should they not be moved spontaneously by the work. The accordion, lying silent on her lap, contributes nothing to the scene except to remind us that music can still be a pleasure to blind people, albeit a pale shade of the visual pleasures afforded us by the artist and, by implication, the visual world. It may also suggest that the girl has to play for a living, thus evoking further pity.

Although the picture does evoke the positive feeling of compassion for the girl, since she is beautiful and wears an expression of tranquility, the over-riding emotion is that of an infinite sadness for someone who can never see what we as viewers can: the rainbows, the birds, the stream, and most poignant of all, her own beauty. Overall, we feel not a healthy regard for someone who is so obviously loved, but sorry for someone who is not as well off as we are. A potentially good emotion is therefore turned into a patronizing one as far as the object of that emotion is concerned, and we are left feeling superior to her and those like her. Instead of admiring or even envying her, we thank our lucky stars that we are not like her, and the next time we see a blind person engaged in fund-raising we put a pound in the tin instead of the customary ten pence.

When we turn to literature and drama we find that they are replete with negative stereotypes of blind people. We read portrayals of blind and visually impaired people as evil and cunning (as in Robert Louis Stevenson's Blind Pew in *Treasure Island*); power-crazed and authoritarian (as in the one-eyed General in Richard Adams' *Watership Down*); helpless, useless and better off dead (as in Kipling's Dick Heldar in *The Light That Failed*); ugly and undesirable (as in D'Annunzio's Anna in the tragic play *The Dead City*), and even as a symbol of death (as in Tennessee Williams' *Streetcar Named Desire*, where the blind flower-seller prefigures Blanche Dubois' physical humiliation and psychological disintegration).

Blindness has also been portrayed as a punishment (as in the blinding of Gloucester in Shakespeare's *King Lear*), and blinding coupled with castration (an ancient and disturbingly symbolic association) was recently shown as the ultimate punishment, humiliation and degradation during press coverage of the Gulf War, giving out the message that when it occurs, it is somehow deserved; a view echoing the fate of Mr Rochester in Charlotte Bronte's *Jane Eyre* (whose sight mysteriously improves as he begins to face his responsibilities!). Such images invite the viewer to hold a moral view of the victim; one in which pity is the only appropriate and indeed possible response for those who are capable of feeling any compassion, and a sense of rightness and finality is the appropriate and equally only possible response for those incapable of, or reluctant to show, compassion.

The above examples represent somewhat superficial or symbolic use of blind characters and of the act of blinding. We need to turn to more serious attempts by sighted writers to depict blindness in order to understand the depths of prejudice held by the author which reveal themselves in the level of characterization achieved. One good example is that of Somerset Maugham's play, *For Services Rendered*, which

has a blind ex-serviceman named Sydney as one of its central
characters. Sydney is portrayed as a person whose sole role
in life is to put up with his blindness. He spends his days
sitting around doing his tatting (making up scraps of material
into something or other), playing the odd game of chess, and
being entertained by those who drift in and out of his long
and empty days. All of his emotional energies are directed
towards bearing the knowledge that he is useless, deserving
of pity and of being regarded as an invalid by those sighted
people around him.

Sydney is particularly sensitive to the fact that he is unable
to engage in gainful employment, and he is made to observe,
with deadly accuracy in his own case, that '. . . being blind
is a full-time occupation in itself'. The message here is that
blind people should not be expected to do anything other than
to devote all their energies into just coping with being blind.
Worse than Sydney's own resignation and despair, however,
are the feelings of his relatives, who are unable to forgive him
for shattering their own hopes for the future, and the resentment on both sides of the dependent relationship is only too
well conveyed in the play.

Lest anyone think that Maugham's play is out of date, let
us consider a more modern example of a sighted scriptwriter's
portrayal of a blind person, because the cinema continues to
fuel sighted people's perceptions that blind people are incompetent to the extent that we can be forgiven for regarding them
as legitimate figures for ridicule. A recent comedy (*sic*!)
screened on television over the Christmas period showed a
young girl wearing bottle-glass spectacles, while she struggles
with a cane and a dog simultaneously, the one getting in the
way of the other, to her considerable discomfiture. She is made
to blunder about, knocking things over, stepping on her guide
dog and so forth. By the middle of the film she has a bucket
of water on each foot; all of this to the obvious merriment
of the sighted people around her. This film was screened at
peak viewing time, and was obviously considered by the television company to be appropriate family entertainment, although
I personally was unable to continue watching it further. If
you should ever find your sensibilities similarly offended,
make sure you write to the Broadcasting Standards Council

or the Broadcasting Complaints Commission to register your distaste.

The media, however, sometimes manage to redress the balance. A recent edition of BBC2's *One in Four*, a disability awareness programme, highlighted the plight of Australian television comic, Andrew Denton, who unwittingly offended a blind member of his audience by accusing her of sleeping through his show. Producing a white cane from her bag, the lady gave back as good as she got. As a result of this mutually humiliating experience, Denton staged a show called *The International Year of the Patronizing Bastard*, which used humour to expose the prejudices of able-bodied people towards disabled individuals. Although some of the studio audience walked out as soon as the show began, the programme did manage to bring home forcibly many issues that can hardly be talked about.

But things are changing. Over the last year or two, disabled people themselves have begun to work creatively through the media to further their causes. For example, the disabled Australian comic, Steady Eddie, whose jokes about what it is like to suffer from cerebral palsy are in the worst possible taste. It is to be hoped that more disabled people will be able to work creatively through the media to educate the public at large about how their behaviour towards disabled people is evaluated by the long-suffering recipients.

As far as portraying accurately the experience of blindness is concerned, on the whole, it has been left to blind authors themselves to convey the realities of sight loss. Unfortunately, such works are hardly ever of the same literary stature as those by sighted authors which portray negative stereotypes, or which attempt to make some general moral point through the vehicle of blindness. They tend rather to be written as factual accounts which try to communicate a unique experience of triumph over adversity, rather than being great works which encompass some universal aspect of the human conditonin a recognized art form.

Recently, however, there have been two notable exceptions to this trend. Hull's book, mentioned earlier, touches on deep, personal meanings which lesser writers have not dared to tackle. Hull explores these meanings as a blind person of great religious faith. He explores the phenomenology and metaphysics of blindness in a painfully honest fashion and concludes that the task of understanding is a difficult and lengthy one. By way of complete contrast, *Snakewalk*, by Charles Wheeler (1989), represents a highly secular account, couched in fiction, of what it is like to be on the receiving end of rehabilitation. Written with a pen dripping with testosterone, Wheeler's book vividly presents an alternative approach to blindness to that of Hull. That such varied responses can be equally valid illustrates the futility of generalizing from one individual's experiences to those of 'the blind', reminding us that blind people are first and foremost individuals in their own right.

Some autobiographies, although aiming to disabuse the reader of the notion of a blind person as helpless and worthy only of pity, unintentionally succeed in portraying blindness as a medical complaint which can be remedied. A revealing title illustrating this medicalization of blindness is that by Thornton (1960), in his autobiography *Cure for Blindness*, which makes for very dated reading today. But however well or badly books about blindness by blind people are written, the classical works portraying negative stereotypes tend to get read more than the true-life accounts and, even more disturbing, these are the very ones which are most likely to appear on school and university syllabuses, thereby perpetuating the institutionalization of prejudice.

The point of highlighting these examples is to show how all the best efforts of rehabilitation workers to foster independence, self-respect and freedom of choice in their clients stand in danger of being undermined by the very attitudes of powerful sectors of our society, even those which may purport to have the interests of blind and visually impaired people at heart. Personal prejudice can very easily become institutionalized discrimination if it is shared by a number of people, and institutionalized discrimination in turn can suggest and reinforce personal prejudice. As advocates for our clients we should be alert to such issues and take every opportunity of rooting out and fighting the enemy within as well as without.

Just as damaging a prejudice as the negative one is the unrealistically positive one, where the blind person is portrayed as some sort of super-hero. Instead of being seen as an object of abject misery, he is seen as someone with miraculous powers, either physical or mental. Science fiction writers often have such characters in their plots, and I have personally met blind people who are seldom out of the limelight. They travel for miles every day, usually by means of a cane, whether they need to go out or not. They jet around the world, hopping on planes as you or I would hop on a bus. They take up some dangerous sport such as hang-gliding or water-skiing. They have a terrific time, and good for them. But one must ask oneself what effect the publicizing of such activities must have on other blind people who do not have the aspirations, the courage or even the means to pursue such exotic pastimes.

We should also consider the effects of those well-meaning, able-bodied people who go out of their way to present images of disabled people's achievements. Hardly a week goes by without the media showing us some person with a disability performing some miraculous feat or other. Whether it is a blind ski-jumper or a bilateral amputee completing a marathon, these images do nothing to change the negative stereotype of disability. We are supposed to be amazed that such things are possible, and we are supposed to be filled with admiration at these achievements. Indeed we are, but why?

Behind these sentiments lurks the old stereotype: disabled people in general cannot or should not be expected to do any of these things. In other words, when we see an example of someone violating the negative expectation it is a case of the exception proving the rule. So the public spectacle of these achievements, whose publicity is calculated to foster positive attitudes towards disabled people, instead reinforces existing stereotypes of low expectations. These, in turn, suggest underachievement to those who happen to have the disability and are trying to overcome its handicapping effects. Thanks to the disability rights movements which have fought for, and won, a certain measure of integration of disabled people into society, the stereotyped images still being purveyed by the able-bodied are at last beginning to be eroded.

TERMINOLOGY

The terms 'disability', 'impairment' and 'handicap' have traditionally been used interchangeably, mainly for stylistic considerations by writers who dislike using the same word twice if a synonym exists. However, in 1980 the World Health Organisation (WHO, 1980) attempted to give these terms strict operational meaning within a framework which was designed to separate them conceptually while linking them theoretically. As a result, we now have an agreed set of principles which help us to keep our thinking clear.

In the first place, according to WHO, there is a disease or a defect which affects an organ. This is a medical condition, and it will have a medical name. For example, if we are talking about a cataract, then this can be identified as a disease or a structural defect in the lens which may be correctable by means of surgery. At the structural level therefore, the professionals involved in intervention are medically qualified people.

A disease or a defect is likely to give rise to an impairment. In the case of the eye, a dislocated lens might interfere with the focusing of light rays on to the retina, thereby impairing the eye's ability to resolve fine detail. At the functional level therefore, the professionals involved in intervention are likely to be orthoptists and opticians, given that there is no possibility of correcting the structural defect at its primary source.

If, after correction, this impairment restricts the person in carrying out activities in the manner or within the range considered to be normal for a human being, then it is considered to be disabling. A disability therefore exists on the level of the personal, and the professionals likely to be involved in intervention are rehabilitation workers, physiotherapists, occupational therapists and the like.

If this disability prevents the person from carrying out a role which would be regarded as normal for them in their everyday lives, then they are said to be handicapped. The key word here is 'role', and this is a sociological term implying the existence of other people playing different or similar roles. A handicap can therefore be seen to be a *social* consequence of a disability, and the professionals likely to be involved in intervention are rehabilitation workers, social workers, psychologists and the like.

When placed in this context it is easy to see why visual impairment can be so handicapping. The simple reason is that we live in a predominantly sighted world which has evolved to serve the needs of sighted people. Sighted people can take in at a glance any changes in the environment such as a door being open as opposed to being shut; a bicycle approaching silently; a car jumping the red traffic light, and so on. Thus sighted people tend to behave in a somewhat casual fashion, relying on this thing called sight to help them out at a moment's notice. Little wonder that visually impaired people are so handicapped by the actions of those who have the luxury of good vision.

In spite of the WHO's attempts to introduce conceptual distinctions and consistent terminology into the field, disabled people themselves have taken issue with an approach which is based ultimately on the medical concept of an incomplete person (Oliver, 1990). To them, a disability (not just a handicap) is a social phenomenon whose causes are not to be identified with structural or functional defects within the individual, but rather with the ways in which society produces disadvantage or restriction on a person who simply happens to be different from the majority, through its unwillingness to make special provision for such people. Viewing a disability as a social phenomenon places the cause, as well as the responsibility for ways of removing the disability, fairly and squarely within society, rather than within the individual who is considered to be suffering from a condition which can be alleviated only by the ministrations of some expert.

A thought experiment

It is interesting to ponder for a moment on the implications of a purely social definition of disability, pausing to carry out a simple thought experiment. Let us imagine that there is a race of people who possess no legs, but who have the ability to design and build turbo-charged wheelchairs. They evolve a system of high-speed, personal transportation consisting of motorways with exit junctions and slip-roads to urban centres.

A human with legs enters this environment and tries to hire a wheelchair. Because he has legs, he cannot fit himself into the only type available, so he reluctantly proceeds on foot. Very soon he gets run over as he attempts to walk across one of the motorways. He curses the people for being so inconsiderate that they see no need for pedestrian under- or over-passes, or even pavements. He discovers that in such a community he is severely handicapped and as a result decides to do something about it.

In hospital, he receives counselling to help him change his attitudes, and as a result he telephones a firm which specializes in modifying wheelchairs, and arranges to visit them. When he arrives, he finds that he cannot get into the shop without going down on his hands and knees, because people who always use wheelchairs build rooms with doorways only four feet high. He persuades the firm to build him a very expensive, custom-made wheelchair which he pays for with a bank loan, and which he collects after waiting for several frustrating weeks. After having received a course of costly tuition and having passed his driving test, he gets onto the nearest motorway and, because he is feeling thirsty, stops off at the first service station for a drink.

Having purchased his drink, he looks around for a vacant table. He finds one, but soon discovers that he cannot sit at it properly because there is no room beneath it to put his legs. He drinks awkwardly and with embarrassment, sitting alongside the table in the passageway, to the obvious irritation of other diners who constantly have to ask him to move in order to get past him. He realizes ruefully that having legs will always place him at a disadvantage in an environment created by those who have none. The thought of booking an appointment with an orthopaedic surgeon to have his legs amputated vaguely crosses his mind ...

In this chapter we have looked at ways in which blindness has been construed within our culture, and how handicapping images of blindness are readily available with which we can identify. These images are available to us all as we construct our roles in life. In the absence of first-hand experience with a person, we act out a role in relation to them which we believe is appropriate for us, given our perception of their role.

If that role is a handicapping one, then we can enter into a collusion in which we reinforce one another's behaviour. If others are a witness to our performances then we advertise the appropriateness of these roles by giving them a first-hand experience which supports, strengthens and perpetuates the stereotype with which we all began.

The following chapters present a number of themes which, taken individually, might appear somewhat disparate, but it is the intention to explicate as many of the factors which impinge upon a client's life as possible. These range from the physiological, through the psychological, right through to the political, and they are presented here in order to enable the helping professionals to do the maximum justice to the opportunity each of you has been given to contribute to those whose lives may have been shattered by events beyond their control.

Some people never really manage to come to terms completely with their sight loss, remaining, like Sydney in Somerset Maugham's play, to a greater or lesser degree dependent upon others for the rest of their lives, and feeling as bitter and resentful towards these people as they feel towards them. Others appear to have done so remarkably well, with only the occasional lapse into self-pity or anger engendered by frustration. Others still use the event in a positive way and go on to achieve more than they would ever have done if they still had sight, or to find some deep, religious meaning in their loss. But however the individual construes their predicament, sight loss presents them with a stark set of choices, many of which do not become apparent for some considerable time after sight has gone and the shock of no longer seeing has passed. Your job is to help make the implications of these choices clear and to support your client in making the best ones available, rather than allowing them to go for the initially easy option of dependency with its long-term disadvantages.

2

Models of rehabilitation

Independence training is an activity in which professionals such as Occupational Therapists (OTs) have been engaged for many years. Although OTs have not routinely been involved in the rehabilitation of blind and partially sighted people in the United Kingdom, they are in other countries. There are many concepts in theories of occupational therapy treatment which run parallel to those in theories of the rehabilitation of visually impaired people, and workers such as Trombly (1983) have outlined a number of main approaches to occupational therapy. Two of those are worth considering in relation to rehabilitation work, because they help us to understand the range of problems and solutions which rehabilitation can encompass.

The first is known as the rehabilitative approach, and this is characterized by the fact that it considers the capacities of the individual on a number of levels ranging from the physical, through the emotional, the cognitive, the cultural and the vocational, to the environmental. The goal of rehabilitation is to get the recipient to recognize their strengths and limitations, and their psychological adjustment to these. The second is called the humanistic approach and this examines how the individual experiences his environment and to what extent he feels in control of it. The humanistic approach concentrates primarily on the client's self-awareness, his attitudes towards himself and others, and his moods. There is therefore some overlap between the two approaches.

From the point of view of current rehabilitation practices I would suggest that we need to consider all of the factors present in both of these models in order to do justice to the range of problems experienced by blind and visually impaired people. Useful as Trombly's scheme is, it has to be recognized that the problems facing the rehabilitation worker in visual impairment necessitate a broadly based approach. The model put forward throughout this book will therefore exemplify practice based upon a combination of the rehabilitative and the humanistic, and each reader will be able to evaluate for herself to what extent she is already implementing them in her action programme.

The ways in which rehabilitation specialists are trained varies enormously between countries and these differences in training largely determine the role model for the rehabilitation specialist. In the United States, students have to have attended college before being able to enter a Master's programme in Orientation and Mobility (O & M). Once they have completed their training, they must then complete a probationary period before becoming eligible for certification. They therefore spend a number of years in training before becoming fully qualified. During the course of their studies, these students will have covered many specialized topics such as anatomy and physiology of the eye; neuropsychology; abnormal psychology; social psychology; health studies; the biomechanics of locomotion; the causes and treatment of various additional handicaps, along with their practical training in the techniques of orientation and mobility.

The range of subjects studied reflects the belief that rehabilitation is a multidisciplinary task, and that the rehabilitation specialist needs to have a wide as well as an in-depth range of knowledge from a number of different disciplines. The American model of training is therefore analogous to the way in which medical practitioners are trained: first of all, a number of relevant subjects are studied, followed by a specialization in one, culminating in a period of practising under probationary conditions before the individual can be regarded as fully competent.

In the United Kingdom, rehabilitation specialists have traditionally been trained in two ways. The first is in long-cane training, and such people used to be called Mobility Officers. The second is in independent living skills (formerly known as daily living skills) training, and such people used to be called Technical Officers. Technical Officers were formerly known as

Home Teachers, and their job was to impart indoor mobility, communication and personal care skills to their clients. They were trained by the Regional Associations for the Blind before outdoor mobility instruction was introduced into the country.

It is interesting to note that the term 'rehabilitation' was not in general use at that time. The word 'welfare' was commonly used to cover all aspects of intervention with blind people, and the connotation of the word suggests that the primary concern was with the individual's well-being, both in the material and the spiritual sense. It is also interesting to note that establishments which now call themselves rehabilitation centres used to have names like 'Homes for Recovery', where the recently blinded (usually war-blinded) client could simply sit around in nice surroundings, gaining comfort and strength from sympathetic staff and balmy air.

With the advent of mobility training in the 1960s, a new breed of professional was thus introduced into blind people's lives. Traditionally, the training for the Technical Officer's role had taken six months. On the basis of this precedent, the training for the Mobility Officer was based on elements of the mobility specialization which were imported from the United States, and a training centre in Birmingham was established, soon to become known as the National Mobility Centre. The adequacy of the resulting training was monitored during the early years by the Blind Mobility Research Unit at the University of Nottingham, which has been conducting research into blindness and visual impairment ever since.

Towards the end of the 1980s, it was considered that it would be better if the separate roles of the Mobility Officer and the Technical Officer were combined into that of one person to be known as a Rehabilitation Worker. On the basis of this thinking, the Regional Associations for the blind, together with the National Mobility Centre and the Guide Dogs for the Blind Association began to run a one year's training course for Rehabilitation Workers. This course combined elements of mobility and daily living skill training with more general topics related to health studies, social work and psychology, and a training board was set up to monitor the content of these courses and to pursue a means of national accreditation. At the time of writing, this has not yet been achieved.

Therefore, today there are two very different levels of professional who come into contact with blind people, depending upon which side of the Atlantic or the Pacific they live. On the one hand, there are those who have trained in depth in a number of distinct academic disciplines, and on the other there are those who have learned how to practise the skills which they then teach, combined with a general background in related topics. It is hardly surprising that the two sorts of professional, the O & M specialist in the United States and Australia, and the Rehabilitation Worker in the United Kingdom, should often find it difficult to communicate with one another, and there is still much debate as to the level of academic training required by someone whose main concern is at the practical rather than at the theoretical level.

TO SEE OR NOT TO SEE?

Before leaving the issue of training, perhaps we should consider what competencies are required for someone to be allowed to call herself an O & M Instructor, or a Rehabilitation Worker. In spite of the existence of national accreditation, there are people in the United States who are working as O & M practitioners without certification. These people cannot ever become certificated as they are themselves visually impaired. The reason for this situation is that the National Accreditation Council's criteria of competence include a number of skills which only a fully sighted person can possess, such as being able to monitor a client's progress at a distance.

Although this state of affairs has been regarded by some people as discriminatory, it has not changed the views of those responsible for the accreditation process. Nor has it stopped those visually impaired people from continuing to work as O & M instructors. At a seminar at the Royal National Institute for the Blind (RNIB) (Dodds, 1984), the present author presented his observations of mobility instruction by blind people, and concluded that one could not really justify the claim that being blind in principle prevented an instructor from teaching other, totally blind people long cane. On the other hand, it must be recognized that such people do have rare talents and determination, and that not every visually impaired person should consider employment as a rehabilitator simply because they have a visual impairment.

Although one can understand the reasons why sighted instructors should be apprehensive about blind instructors, it is curious that those who believe so much in the long cane system, and have such faith in it for their clients, feel the need to undermine that belief by preventing blind people from imparting to other blind people the skills upon which their own lives depend. One would have thought that a blind person who used her cane every day would have more understanding of the environment as experienced by her client than would a sighted instructor, and this conjecture is borne out in the following anecdote based upon first-hand experience.

When the present author visited the Social Services for the Blind in Nebraska, he had the opportunity of being taught under blindfold by a blind instructor. During the lesson, we walked under what sounded like a railway bridge, and the instructor reinforced my perceptions when she debriefed me after the lesson. On the way into the centre, we met a sighted instructor about to take out her client. We talked about the route which I had just completed, and the sighted instructor seemed surprised to hear about the railway bridge, of whose existence she had been unaware.

Following the subsequent, friendly disagreement, I decided to retrace the route with my blindfold removed. On arriving at the point where I thought that I had heard the bridge, I was surprised to find that there was none. However, on looking more closely at the situation, it was clear to me that there had once been a railway bridge there, but that the bridge had been removed, leaving only the buttresses. Visually, there was no bridge, but auditorily there was. This explained why the blind instructor's perceptions differed from those of the sighted instructor, but as far as the client was concerned, the blind instructor, by virtue of inhabiting the same perceptual world as her client, had been more helpful than the sighted instructor. This observation led me to believe that blind instructors had more to offer than perhaps had been considered, and this issue will be touched upon again in Chapter 8 in relation to teaching styles.

Following the RNIB seminar, training agencies in the United Kingdom are now accepting students with a visual disability for training as Rehabilitation Workers, although no-one has had the courage of their convictions in training a totally blind instructor. Perhaps this is because no-one really knows how to go about training a blind person to teach mobility, although the same reservations do not seem to hold true of daily living or communication skills. But one has to acknowledge that a blind instructor working in a local authority would require a driver, and it may be that this is the real reason for the lack of interest in training blind people to become Rehabilitation Workers, particularly if mobility instruction is seen to be a major part of their work. Also, a blind instructor would need to spend much longer assessing routes near clients' homes during domiciliary training, and this could be the major hurdle. But as far as residential rehabilitation is concerned, such problems need not arise.

ROLES WHICH THE REHABILITATOR MAY ADOPT

In order to know how to relate to her client, the rehabilitator will have to have some idea of the goals which she wishes the client to attain. She will then have to choose a role which fits in with achieving these goals. In short, she will have to develop a helping model, or a philosophy of intervention which does justice to the relevant factors (Lang, van der Molen, Trower *et al.*, 1990). Unfortunately, it is not easy to pin down with any degree of precision the range of goals and roles which are involved in the process of rehabilitation. The ultimate goal is for the client to become as independent as he needs or wishes to be, but this distant goal needs to be broken down into more specific and short-term goals in order for the rehabilitation to proceed. Once these have been considered, a number of possible roles emerge, and it might be worth considering them one by one.

Technician

In the first place, let us consider the role of the worker as technician. Technicians are people who are trained in various ways of dealing with instruments of one sort or another. The long cane may be regarded as one such instrument, along with the panoply of gadgets available for activities of daily living, and the techniques for using these are something which the rehabilitation worker has at her fingertips, so to speak. With the advent of microcomputers, the range of technological solutions to the problems of blindness and partial sight has burgeoned, and with it, the need for the rehabilitation worker to come to grips with some quite sophisticated technology. It is probably fair to say that at present few workers find themselves in a position of competence to handle a number of the more advanced devices and equipment available on the market, particularly those which facilitate information storage and transfer, and it is invariably left to the distributors of such equipment to provide demonstration and training.

This state of affairs is unfortunate, because the cost of providing such a service greatly adds to the cost of the equipment, and the cost of service contracts often needs to be further added. In an attempt to keep costs down and make equipment available at a competitive price, few manufacturers are able to provide the introductory demonstration and back-up which would help ensure an awareness and an uptake of their product. This often means that an otherwise good product fails to take off because potential purchasers are afraid to make a commitment to something of which they and their rehabilitation worker may be equally ignorant or apprehensive. There is an urgent need for those responsible for the training of rehabilitation workers to provide their students with access to the latest technology, together with training in its use, if the maximum availability and consequent benefit from such technology can be obtained.

Teacher

Rehabilitation involves learning a wide range of skills which have to be taught. So that teaching skills are essential components of the rehabilitation process. The role of teacher should therefore be considered, and the two philosophies of teaching which have been characterized as 'filling vessels' and 'lighting candles'. The former assumes that the pupil's mind is like a blank slate, and that the teacher's role is to fill the mind with information. The latter assumes that the learner's mind will be stimulated into making connections between facts once they have been given.

The term 'instructor' implicitly assumes that the client is simply shown what to do, and that after having had the opportunity of putting a number of specific techniques into practice, he can be trusted to his own devices. The old label 'Mobility Officer' also conjures up the image of a person whose task it is to drill into the client the various skills of independent mobility. Nowadays, educational theory stresses the need to arouse interest in the learner, a view much closer to the idea of lighting candles. Additionally, since one–to-one teaching is the rule in rehabilitation work, the role of the rehabilitation worker is largely to structure the learner's experiences in a systematic way so that the client can discover for himself how the time-honoured techniques can provide safety and independence.

In particular, in adult education it has to be recognized that the learner's mind is not a blank slate by any stretch of the imagination, and there there is already perhaps half a lifetime's experience accumulated in it, representing an elaborate model of the world and how the person himself fits into it. The role of the rehabilitation worker as teacher is to capitalize on the person's interests, abilities and aspirations, and to modify them where appropriate. In order to do this, she must negotiate the various rehabilitation goals with the client in order that they should have relevance to his own plans for his life, or re-negotiate the client's own model of his relationship to the world now that he is no longer predominantly a sighted person.

Mentor

Because one's client is likely to become demoralized at certain points in their training, one of the roles which the rehabilitation worker must adopt is that of mentor. A mentor is someone who cares for the client, and takes care of their progress through the various stages of learning, keeping up his morale or coaxing him to try new things. By acting as mentor you will ensure that the client gets the most out of your teaching, and you will be able to guide the client through what could otherwise be a painful learning process so that he does not experience unnecessary setbacks or emotional shocks.

To be a good mentor requires considerable experience and maturity, and those of you who have just begun your careers probably recognize it in more senior workers, but do not yet recognize it in yourselves. Only the passage of time will bring about such a confidence, but by paying attention to when you feel you may have got it wrong, rather than blotting such episodes out of your mind, and by making a mental note to do things differently in the future, you will hasten the development of this aspect of yourself. Never assume that you are right and the client is wrong when things do not work out. Always ask yourself, 'What else might I have done?' or 'How else could I have gone about that?'

Coach

Although mobility is not generally regarded as a sport, O & M instructors are required to train under blindfold in order to become proficient at the skills which they then have to teach. This model corresponds loosely to that involved in coaching. Coaches are traditionally sportsmen or women who are past the age at which they can excel at their sport, but who through their experience possess a special understanding of the problems involved in performing at high levels of skill, and hence can be considered to be in a good position to help those less skilled than they themselves once were.

Coaches can often spot a problem which an individual is experiencing, and offer suggestions as to how to eradicate it. They can compare their pupils' performance with that of their own, and make suggestions as to how to bring about an improvement. These suggestions can vary from the adoption of a different technique to the adoption of a different attitude of mind: the value of mental training is also recognized, and coaches can often diagnose faulty thinking as well as faulty technique. By virtue of the Rehabilitation Worker's experience under blindfold, she is able to enter the client's mental world in a way which, say, a psychologist is unable, and because of her proficiency at the task she can also put on a blindfold and experience the problems encountered by her client.

Counsellor

Many clients come to you in a distressed condition, and although most of your training will have prepared you to give them specific independence skills, you are likely to find yourself responding on an emotional level to their distress. Some of you may feel as much like crying for the client as the client feels like crying for himself, and this shows a well-developed sense of empathy which will take care of the ways in which you go about teaching your client. But not all people have the ability to get under the client's skin to such an extent, and others of you may have to protect your own feelings by refusing to identify too closely with those of your client.

One aspect of your interaction with the client may therefore be to deal directly with the feelings with which you are being confronted. This requires that you take on the role of counsellor, in which many of you may have received training. Those of you who have not had formal training in any aspect of counselling may nonetheless behave as a counsellor just by virtue of the fact that you are a human being who is part of the same human condition as your client. But counselling can take many forms, so that it is important to recognize this before embarking on it, and to obtain some form of recognized qualification in counselling if you feel that there is a need for those sorts of skill.

Part of counselling involves giving the client and their family information which will help them to understand why they may be feeling as they do, or how long they are likely to feel the way they do. Another aspect of your role as counsellor may be to explore feelings which make the client confused, and to negotiate a meaning in the client's chaotic emotional life. You may need to involve other members of the family and deal with their feelings towards the client, which may not coincide with yours. In this way you can get the family to come to express their hopes and fears in a way which is constructive and which will not impede your progress with the client once the rehabilitation programme gets under way. These considerations form the basis of Chapter 9.

Many workers are taught that depressed clients are grieving for their lost sight and that grief counselling and therapy are appropriate. Although it may indeed be true that a client is sad at the loss of a number of features of his life which he valued, one need not construe this as grief. Chapter 3 offers a critique of the loss model and the reader is advised to consider the arguments presented before deciding upon whether or not to proceed along the lines of grief counselling.

Psychologist

Having to learn a completely new way of going about one's life is very threatening. Most people respond to enforced change with fear and attempts to avoid having to make any change if at all possible. One of your tasks is to turn what may be perceived as threats into challenges for your client. For example, the whole idea of walking alone alongside a busy main road may terrify someone who is currently unable to take even two steps confidently inside their own familiar home surroundings. Similarly, the thought that he might be expected to cook a meal without any assistance may fill the client with misgivings.

Although you may not be a psychologist, part of your job is to present the various independent living tasks in such a way that your client warms to the idea of having a go. You must convey the attitude that your expectation of him to succeed at the wide range of tasks with which you are going to present him is a realistic one based on your experiences with other clients. You need to allay his fears and present the learning in a way which challenges him without being threatening. You need to offer emotional support when required, and generally keep track of his morale. If you lose touch with your client's state of mind, you will do him less than optimal service.

However, unless you have received some form of training in clinical psychology or advanced counselling, try to resist the temptation to engage in any sort of therapeutic intervention with a client. Clients who are suffering from depression and anxiety need to be referred to the appropriate professional, although you can help to alleviate many symptoms of depression by giving the client your undivided attention, moral support and simple kindness; and anxiety can be reduced substantially by giving information which can reduce the client's apprehensiveness. Ways in which you can help your client to deal with the emotional aspects of sight loss are discussed in detail in Chapters 3 and 8.

Advocate

Yet another role which you may need to take with respect to your client is that of advocate. Families often try to take power away from a person once they have lost their sight, and they may do this quite unconsciously. Alternatively, they may consciously believe that their insistence on doing everything for the client is an appropriate expression of their affection. Although help and support are certainly needed in the early stages of adjustment, by the time you have begun your intervention it is time for this to be reduced and replaced by more behaviour from the client and less from others.

In order to achieve this you may have to stick up for your client when people act in a way which tends to make your job more difficult. It is not only members of the family who can negate your best efforts to impart independence; members of the public can also attempt to pervert the course of rehabilitation. For example, a shopkeeper may have goods displayed on the pavement which pose a hazard to your client, or a passer by might remark angrily, as one did to me once, that you are expecting your client to do the impossible. Deal with these situations with courtesy and calm, even although you might be seething inside. Always justify your actions with a rational explanation which does not threaten the other party, and even in cases of unreasonable behaviour try to see the other person's point of view while persuading them that yours is equally valid. If you find that you have difficulty in doing this, consider attending a course on assertiveness training.

Friend

Given that independence training is conducted on a one–to–one basis, and that the rehabilitation worker spends much of her time dealing with personal and private matters, we have to consider that some of the time you are acting as a genuine friend to someone in need. Not that you will feel this way towards all of your clients, but you may genuinely like some of your clients and feel an affinity with them. This means that boundaries of intimacy need to be negotiated. Ideally, the client should be allowed to set these boundaries, but some may not wish to set any, in which case it is up to you to make clear what is and what is not permitted. It should also be understood that most clients are very vulnerable when they come for rehabilitation, and that they may encourage a level of intimacy which satisfies their emotional needs but which encourages you to step beyond the boundaries of your professional role.

All research into the effects of physical intimacy between helper and client has invariably shown that any physical contact beyond a genuine hug or holding of hands in times of despair tends to favour a poor outcome for the client. This is mainly because greater levels of intimacy encourage dependency, whereas the goal of rehabilitation is independence. But you will all at some time in your careers find yourself faced with the dilemma: 'Should I or shouldn't I?' The answer is always the same: 'You shouldn't' but it does happen, although being aware of when you might be in danger of crossing the boundary should help you to remain in your professional role. The bottom line, of course, is that even if you both feel it helped, your employer is unlikely to take the same view should he or she discover it. And a plea of mutual help is unlikely to be regarded as a mitigating circumstance surrounding such behaviour at an industrial tribunal. Those of you who may be interested in a comprehensive account of ethics in the helping professions might like to read Corey, Corey and Callanan (1984).

PLAYING THE VARIOUS ROLES

Now that we have seen the various roles which you may have to adopt, you yourself must devise the best ways in which you can do justice to the key elements of each in your dealings with your client. Perhaps you already have a way of doing justice to many of them, but there is no theory available nor even a set of guidelines to help you if you have not. Perhaps one should think of oneself initially as more of a counsellor and potential friend than anything else. Once skill learning is under way you will be predominantly teacher and mentor, with the occasional lapse back into counsellor when setbacks are encountered. If you and your client hit it off, you can regard yourselves as friends, and you will probably wish to keep in touch with one another after training has finished.

When you find a client who does not appear to show much interest in the various rehabilitation tasks, you may have to play psychologist, engineering his motivation by getting him to do something at which he can have some success, and praising him when he does succeed. Above all, you need to give him the message that you expect him to attempt the tasks you set him and, further, that you believe that he will succeed at them. Never take no for an answer, and be prepared to be firm with a client who may try to take advantage of his greater age by trying to tell you that what you are asking of him is unrealistic, or that you do not know what you are talking abut.

The appropriate time to play the role of advocate should be obvious, but try to have a prepared piece rehearsed in anticipation of specific, recurring incidents. It is easy to miss an opportunity simply because one does not quite know how to handle a situation which may arise. Having a stock of arguments ready to hand will free your mind to concentrating on how best to put them forward in a potentially heated moment. Do not be surprised if you find yourself having to play advocate for the client in the face of prejudices expressed or shown by himself and other members of the family. You may know what blind people are capable of, but most people do not. Tell them that you know best, and then go on to prove your point.

In this chapter we have examined models of rehabilitation practice and the various roles which the Rehabilitation Worker needs to adopt at various stages in the rehabilitative process. As technician, you can ensure that he has the most suitable devices available. As teacher you can impart practical skills in an imaginative way. As mentor you can keep a caring and watchful eye on him. As coach, you will know how to get the best performance out of him. As counsellor you can assist his adjustment and give him positive ways of coping with the demands placed upon him. As psychologist you can present the whole series of tasks in a way which maintains his interest and morale. As advocate you can be assertive on his behalf.

As friend you can exchange confidences and talk over intimate issues. If you are already doing most of these things, congratulate yourself: now you know why you feel so tired at the end of the day! If you are not doing all of these things, then by the time you have finished this book you will be in a better position to do justice to the complex task of rehabilitation.

3

Psychological adjustment to sight loss

Once an individual has been registered as a visually impaired or blind person, there is a period of time during which the initial shock accompanying such a radical change of status is gradually replaced by a realization that life will never be the same again. Since loss of sight affects the individual on a number of levels simultaneously, demanding that the ways in which the person perceives, behaves, thinks and feels about things must change, the process of adjustment can be a protracted one, and it may take a number of different courses, depending upon the person's temperament, their previous experiences of setbacks, and their ways of coping with a crisis (Dodds, 1991a). A good account of the practical challenges in adjusting to sight loss is given by Conyers (1992), and the following presents a theoretical model which is intended to provide a balance to more traditional views.

The term 'coping' is one of whose use is unfortunately inversely related to its precision (Filipp, Aymanns and Braukmann, 1986), and it has been used in a multiplicity of ways to refer to a wide range of phenomena. Psychologists have not contributed much to an understanding of the practicalities of coping, tending instead to concentrate on abstract descriptions of a range of processes which do not really help the practitioner. In essence, coping refers to the ability of the person to reduce the mismatch between the resources at his disposal and the demands made upon him. Coping with sight loss has to take place on the perceptual, the behavioural, the cognitive and the emotional levels, and these are closely inter-related to one another. Good practical accounts of coping with disability and sight loss are to be found in Isherwood (1986) and Hutchinson (1991), and a number of techniques which can help to reduce stress are dealt with more fully in Chapter 8.

The term 'adjustment' is also one which has not been considered very carefully, if at all, by those who use it, and yet it is a central concept in rehabilitation. It is probably regarded as the 'hidden agenda' in all rehabilitation pro-grammes, although it may not be recognized explicitly by workers who are not trained psychologists. Nonetheless, most practitioners will already be aware of the importance of acknowledging their clients' emotional and mental states, and will proceed with care and caution if they perceive that a client needs special consideration. Existing models of adjustment tend to be based on some model of bereavement and loss (Pitts, 1991), although as we shall see later, such models are highly questionable.

In his autobiography, Hull (1990) outlines four distinct stages in his own adjustment to sight loss. The first was a period of hope, which lasted between one year and 18 months, during which the finality of sight loss had not been accepted. The next phase consisted of what appeared on the surface to be quite positive behaviour: the search for alternative techniques and the re-equipping of an office, but this phase was to be replaced by a period of despair, characterized by sleeplessness and depression which lasted for a year. The final period was an emergence from this despair into a realization that there were many inner strengths, although the process of adjustment was by no means yet over.

A major part of the rehabilitation worker's job is to give her client the emotional as well as the practical support necessary to overcome the fears and misgivings which invariably accom-pany such major losses of competence, and the depression which can often overwhelm even the strongest personalities. Although most rehabilitation workers understand the need to acknowledge their clients' thoughts and feelings, few have been given the specialized training which could place their interventions within an accepted psychological framework. While a gramme of common sense is worth a kilogramme of theory, common sense can lack coherence without a conceptual framework, so that it is worthwhile trying to understand the experience of being rendered sightless in the context of mainstream psychological thinking. Also, not all people possess that which is recognized as common sense, a commodity which even experience of life cannot guarantee.

At a common sense level it is easy to see that many clients are very 'down' in their spirits, or may appear to be in 'a bit of a state'. The first handshake can often give this away: a cold, clammy and limp hand can reveal your client's emotional status better than any other outward signs. Many clients will say that they feel useless and worthless, and that it would be best for everyone if they did away with themselves. Many of them fail to show any interest in acquiring new skills, and lack any confidence in their ability to change things for the better. They may tell you that you are wasting your time with them and that you would be better spending it with other people who might benefit from your help. This response forces you into the role of amateur psychologist in that you have to find ways of persuading the client that his views are wrong, and that entertaining them is handicapping his acquisition of independence skills.

ANXIETY AND DEPRESSION

Emotional states such as anxiety and depression are common in people who have recently experienced sight loss. In common sense parlance, anxious people are said to be 'uptight'. On the other hand, 'being down' is what people say they are when psychologists call them depressed. Being depressed is an emotional state, the opposite of which is being euphoric. Neither is a normal emotional state, and neither is desirable because the individual is unable to make sound judgments when in extremes of mood. Depressed people are pessimistic and make gloomy predictions about their futures; euphoric people are wildly optimistic and believe that they can make all their dreams come true. People in neither state are more likely to be realistic and able to make sound judgments about the future. Some people tend to have swings of mood, and as a consequence they are unpredictable to those around them, unless the latter know them well, in which case they will simply be regarded as being in 'one of their moods', and no-one will take their unduly optimistic or pessimistic statements too seriously, knowing that their present mood will soon enough give way to a different one.

As well as being depressed, many blind people are simultaneously anxious. This combination of anxiety and depression can make them physically lethargic but mentally highly active. They may be unable to sleep because their minds are buzzing with unanswered questions, unexpressed hopes and fears, and a real dread for the future. They may be so preoccupied with these thoughts that they appear to have little or no spare attentional capacity to devote to listening to what you or anyone else may have to say to them. They may nod and agree with your suggestions, but if you ask them what you said to them 20 minutes ago they are unlikely to be able to tell you. They may feign interest out of courtesy, but their hearts and minds are not with you and they give the impression of being in another world. For this reason it is important that any information given to a person with recent sight loss is repeated at least once on separate occasions in order to make sure that the message has really sunk in.

Anxiety and depression need not go together, but in the case of sight loss they usually do, and it is easy to understand why this should be so. Loss of sight means that previous ways of going about things are no longer appropriate, so that people cannot cope with the previously normal demands of life by responding automatically; every little thing has to be considered anew. Even simple tasks may now appear monumentally difficult, daunting or dangerous. With only negative stereotypes of blindness to hand, many individuals fear the worst, such as a lifetime of dependency and uselessness, so that they can become very anxious about their current situation and unsure about how they can cope with their changed status. Additionally, the belief that the situation may not improve significantly in the foreseeable future can often bring hopelessness and depression in its wake.

Depression and light

Although there are clearly psychological factors at work in the development of depression consequent upon sight loss, it is only comparatively recently that anyone has suggested that there could be a physiological basis for it. Yet recent research has shown that depression can result from lack of exposure to light (Rosenthal, Sack, Gillin *et al.*, 1984). Mild depression known as 'seasonal affective disorder' (SAD) is experienced by large numbers of people during the winter months, and replacement light therapy has been shown to be effective in combating it (Wehr, Skwere, Jacobson *et al.*, 1987). Light affects the brain in two ways. One is directly via pathways emanating from the optic nerve, the other is via the secretion of a hormone known as melatonin, which is produced in the brain in response to light.

Melatonin is one factor which determines our circadian rhythm (*circa* – about; *diem* – a day), which is another name for our sleep–wake cycle. Many blind people experience a disruption of their circadian rhythms, and melatonin replacement therapy has been found to be effective in restoring them to normal. Perhaps the chronic depression observed in many blind people is linked to the fact that their brains can no longer be affected by light, so that the possibility exists that part of the depression may indeed be physiologically based. Such a speculation needs testing by research, but case studies do indicate that there could well be a link between sight loss and emotional disorder (Paramore and King, 1989; Rosenthal, Della Bella, Hahn *et al.*, 1989), and therapy consisting of exposure to bright light has been found to be effective in such cases.

Depression and attention

Another factor which does not appear to have been taken sufficiently into account when trying to understand depression following visual loss is the effect of sight loss on attentional mechanisms. When vision and another sense such as hearing or touch are put into conflict, vision tends to win over the other sense (Rock and Victor, 1963). This shows how much of our attention is normally taken up by visual input. When a person loses their sight, they also lose the visual input which would normally take up their attention, and this leaves their attention free to monitor input from other channels.

However, if little sense can be made of this information, or if it should be lacking, attention is then likely to turn to bodily sensations or to thoughts and feelings arising from inside, as opposed to outside the person. So if that a person who loses his sight remains highly vigilant to sensory and other inner events such as memories or thoughts, then it is not surprising that he may end up dwelling on inner experiences instead of turning his attention outwards to the external world. If left to his own devices, this can easily become a habit of mind, resulting in withdrawal and a reluctance to engage with the outside world.

SELF-ESTEEM

As well as being anxious and depressed, many clients suffer a catastrophic loss of self-esteem. Given the social stigma of being labelled blind, this is hardly surprising, yet some people manage to retain their self-esteem whereas others lose it, and one might ask why this should be so. According to Cooper-smith (1967), self-esteem has two main origins: one is a sense of self-worth acquired through being loved and accepted during childhood, the other is via a sense of competence acquired during adulthood. Perhaps it is those who lack an early sense of self-worth who lose the most self-esteem as a direct result of sight loss, because their self-esteem depends more upon current levels of competence than early experiences of affection and acceptance. If this should be the case, then it should be possible to restore self-esteem by increasing competence at a wide range of independent living tasks.

Self-esteem has long been realized to be implicated in the adjustment process; so much so that one author has devoted an entire book to it (Tuttle, 1984). Self-esteem is just one aspect of what psychologists have called 'self-image', and we have seen how social images of blind people can shape people's self-images once they have become labelled 'blind'. Some people who lose their sight have such a lost sense of self-esteem that one could say that they actively loathe themselves. Such clients may try to do away with themselves, so that it is important that these people are identified and given special help via counselling, possibly combined with medication in the short term. In residential rehabilitation centres such clients should be observed discreetly but regularly, and they should certainly not be left alone and unoccupied for long periods of time.

SELF-EFFICACY AND LOCUS OF CONTROL

Two concepts central to understanding the process of adjust-ment are self-efficacy (Bandura, 1977) and locus of control (Rotter, 1966). Self-efficacy is simply a subjective estimation of one's likelihood of succeeding or failing at a task with which one is presented. People with a high sense of self-efficacy believe that they are likely to succeed, so that they set about the task quickly and confidently. People with a low sense of self-efficacy believe that they are likely to fail, so that they will try to avoid it in some way or other, or announce in advance that they are likely to fail, so that there is little point in trying.

Similarly, people vary in the degree to which they believe events are within or without their control. People who believe that their behaviour can change things are said to have an internal locus of control, and they are the sort of people who will seldom take no for an answer and who remain persistent in the face of opposition. On the other hand, people who believe that things change only as a result of good or bad luck, or to forces beyond them, are said to have an external locus of control, and such people tend to back off when their efforts do not appear to produce results. They can be characterized as being fatalistic, and tend to come across as passive people.

Self-efficacy and locus of control can therefore be seen to be closely related, although they have arisen from different origins in the literature. Self-efficacy may be regarded as being a task-specific appraisal of the immediate future, whereas locus of control can be considered to be a more general feeling of whether or not one is in the driving seat in life. Research has shown how powerful these psychological mechanisms are in determining whether a person is likely to act positively to make things happen, or whether they are likely to sit around avoiding action for fear of failure. Such a strategy as the latter serves to protect low self-esteem from getting even lower by preventing the anticipated failure from occurring.

One of the most important aspects of self-efficacy and locus of control is that they can both be modified on the basis of outcome. If a person with a low sense of self-efficacy is allowed to have some success, then this raises efficacy expectations for future tasks. By the same token, if a person sees that their actions can have an effect on the outside world, then their sense of control can become more internal. The old adage, 'Nothing succeeds like success', shows how embedded such psychological knowledge is in our Western culture, and success is a very strong motivator of attempts to reach even greater goals.

However, the opposite is equally true: repeated failure produces feelings of powerlessness and the belief that no matter what one does, events are really brought about by chance or external forces beyond one's control. Research has shown that if people are given a task at which they are told repeatedly that they have failed, they will tend to give up after the third attempt (Mikulincer, 1988). Perhaps the adage, 'If at first you don't succeed, try, try and try again' recognizes that more than three failures at a task is as much as any human being can cope with. But it is important to recognize how these elementary feelings and beliefs can determine our behaviour when faced with challenges.

LEARNED HELPLESSNESS

The opposite of feeling in control or efficacious is feeling helpless. Helplessness can be induced experimentally in animals by giving them no opportunity to escape from an aversive situation on a number of repeated occasions, and then presenting them with the opportunity, whereupon they will do nothing to help themselves (Seligman, 1975). Learned helplessness has been considered by some workers to produce symptoms of depression, and the learned helplessness theory of depression has been reformulated to take account of the fact that, whereas animals cannot be credited with understanding how the world is constructed beyond their immediate perceptions, human beings do have a model of how things relate to one another, and that these cognitions need to be acknowledged (Abramson, Seligman and Teasdale, 1978).

More recently, the learned helplessness hypothesis has been refined into a 'learned hopelessness' one, and the existence of a sub-type of depression known as hopelessness–depression has been put forward (Abramson, Metalsky and Alloy, 1989). Hopelessness–depression can be characterized by the occurrence of a major, negative life event which is perceived to be global, permanent and beyond the control of the individual.

Those features appear to epitomize the loss of one's sight, and this author believes that the depression found after sudden loss of sight represents a paradigm case of hopelessness–depression rather than a case of grieving for loss: an issue which we shall look at presently.

Since sudden and severe loss of sight deprives the individual of a wide range of competencies which they have possessed since early childhood, accompanying the loss of these competencies is the loss of a sense of control and efficacy. Regarding oneself as incompetent (which is now a true perception) produces a massive loss of self-esteem, combined with feelings of anxiety and depression, since one knows that in order to have any quality of life at all one must be able to act in order to bring about what one wants. Add a dash of negative attitudes towards blind people conditioned by society's stereotypes, and you have a perfect recipe for hopelessness.

ATTRIBUTIONAL STYLE

The revised version of the learned helplessness theory states that people attribute the causes of success or failure to their own efforts, good or bad luck, or to external events beyond their control. People are said to possess an attributional style, that is to say they tend towards a particular type of attribution when things either work out for them or when they do not work out. Which style they tend toward produces predictable effects on their self-efficacy, their locus of control and their self-esteem. For example, some people have an internal attributional style for success and an external one for failure. This means that they take the credit for good outcomes and blame external forces for poor ones. I call this the 'politician's style', because self-esteem is constantly boosted by success while remaining unaffected by failure.

At the other extreme, some people regard good outcomes as being due to circumstances having been right for them, and poor outcomes as being due to their own ineptitude or incompetence. This is a more unfortunate combination of styles as it results in a chronic loss of self-esteem, low self-efficacy and the development of an external locus of control. It is known as a depressogenic (producing depression) attributional style, and I call this the 'I'm one of life's losers' syndrome. I am sure that we can all bring to mind examples of people we know whose personality seems to depend as much upon which attributional style they adopt as it does on other, more traditional 'personality' factors.

Making excuses or blaming others for unfortunate outcomes are such particularly common and effective attributions that we may tend to accept them at face value (Austin, 1962). We also tend to think that they are immutable traits which people are born with, rather than tendencies which might be altered by giving the individual different sorts of feedback contingent upon what they do. People tend to stick with their habitual attributional styles because they reinforce their own views about themselves and the world in general, whether these are positive or negative, but as rehabilitation workers we are in a position to modify our clients' attributions in a number of different ways. These can then alter self-efficacy, locus of control and self-esteem, so that they are simple but powerful tools which we have at our disposal. Clients who habitually make excuses should be confronted with the fact that they are doing so, and be made to accept responsibility for their actions.

ATTITUDES TOWARDS BLINDNESS AND ACCEPTANCE OF SIGHT LOSS

In the first chapter we looked at the variety of negative stereotypes of blindness available in our culture, and it was argued that if a person had subscribed to these stereotypes when they were sighted, then when they became registered as visually impaired themselves they would be likely to take on those stereotypes. Although research into this area has only recently got under way, there is indeed evidence of a strong relationship between a blind person's attitudes toward blind people in general and the degree to which they accept their own lack of sight (Dodds, Bailey, Pearson *et al.*, 1991c).

Although one cannot argue for a causal link between two things which are simply correlated with one another, the establishment of such a link is an important one in that it suggests that a client's acceptance of their sight loss may be amenable to improvement if their views about blind people could be made more positive. On the other hand, one could argue that if they accepted their own sight loss more, their views about blind people would improve, but I would say that it was more important to try to increase their acceptance of their own sight loss than to change their attitudes to blind people in general.

EXISTING MODELS OF ADJUSTMENT

We now have a number of precise psychological terms which will help us to tease out the various strands of adjustment and place them within a coherent model. There are at least two reasons why a clearly articulated model of adjustment is required. In the first place, the term adjustment has been used too loosely and for too long without having been defined in any agreed manner. This enables people to use it to mean anything they like, producing only an illusion of understanding between two workers who may each use it to mean something quite different.

Second, the perceived need for a newly blinded person to go through a period of adjustment has been taken by many to indicate a need to grieve for sight loss. Thus adjustment is redefined as grieving. At the risk of offending workers whose training has led them to accept uncritically the loss model of adjustment, I would like to put forward a different view which I believe does as much justice to the dynamics of the adjustment process as existing loss models. But first, let me state why I believe that a loss model can never be regarded as a true account of what is going on.

My basic objection comes from an analysis of the use of the term 'grieving', and the activities engaged in by those who believe that grieving is a necessary precondition for adjustment to take place. What leads people to claim that a client is grieving is the fact that they are depressed. When questioned, they may admit to thinking about the days when their sight was all right; when they could see their loved ones, and when they could do anything they wanted to. They may feel very sad to realize that these things are no longer possible. They may feel the loss of the sight of those dearest to them very painful, which it may very well be.

However, not all people feel this way, and this must be recognized. For the worker who believes that grieving is essential for proper adjustment, lack of any signs of grief may be taken to indicate that the grief is being 'repressed', only to emerge at a later date. In such a case the worker may initiate some therapeutic procedure designed to uncover the allegedly repressed feelings. Such a procedure would doubtless focus the client's attention on the loss of the sight of loved ones, the loss of desired activities and so on, and offer a language with which to name the feelings of sadness and sorrow produced by such thoughts. The worker would then act in various ways to help the client to come to terms with these feelings, and would claim to have been of therapeutic help when the client began to show signs of optimism.

One can, however, look on such a scenario with quite a different pair of spectacles. Let us suppose that there is no such thing as repressed anything, including grief. If something is not present, why assume that it still has to be there somewhere? This is a common move in psychoanalysis, and it has been readily taken on board fairly uncritically by parapsychiatric people such as counsellors and psychotherapists. But it could be construed as a power move which places the counsellor or therapist in a superior position to the client and makes the claim that he or she knows better than he does. Since this may be what the client wants to hear anyway, it is a move which often works.

If a client should be bold enough to disagree with the therapist, he may be labelled as 'resistant', 'suppressing' or 'denying' his 'real' feelings, or 'lacking insight' into them. Again, such allegations or even accusations are part of the stock-in-trade of therapists who are playing a power game which the client can win only by quitting therapy and going to a place where they do not have to collude in such degrading games, such as down the pub. Those of you who may feel outraged by such suggestions should read Howarth's (1989) short review of the evidence, or Masson's (1990) polemic; each of which criticize psychoanalytic practice and psychotherapy from very different perspectives, and Haley's (1963) view of psychoanalysis as a special form of one-upmanship is still hard to reject.

The point which I am taking pains to make is that by engaging in any kind of grief work with your client you may run the risk of producing the very feelings which grief theory requires for its existence. Once you have labelled the client's deep, but perhaps vague distress, you may believe that you have helped him come to terms with hidden feelings, now precisely identified and 'worked through'. But it is likely that you will have done nothing more than to negotiate, to a greater or a lesser degree, what language game is appropriate between yourself and your client. Because you have the experience as well as the power, clients will tend to agree with your conceptual framework, particularly since they are unlikely to have a better one of their own.

Although my own arguments against the loss model are based upon logical analysis (Dodds, 1989; 1991a), other workers such as Inde (1988) have found that the loss model does not correspond with their own extensive experience in the field. According to Inde, 'It (the loss model) was like a play, but there was no reality to it'. Inde's choice of words is illuminating, because psychoanalytic theory has undoubtedly contributed more to drama and to literature than it has to any testable model of mental life; more to our imagining of what might be in the mind as opposed to what really is in it. But ideas in themselves tend to take on a life of their own, and if a model can never be refuted by any evidence one way or the other then it is likely to stay around for as long as it appears attractive.

This is undoubtedly one of the reasons why there are over 100 identifiably different types of therapy currently in existence and why no-one will ever be able to tell which, if any, is more effective than any other. Although most people seem to need to believe in something, perhaps we should recognize that as responsible practitioners we should work only with ideas which can be tested for their effectiveness. An alternative model which I would like to present combines the factors identified above, but before spelling it out, let us look at a recent development in psychological thinking which places emotions in the context of conscious thought processes, rather than on hidden mechanisms.

COGNITIONS AND EMOTIONS

It will come as no surprise to anyone that what goes on inside our heads is some combination of thoughts and feelings. The question is, do thoughts produce or elaborate upon feelings, or do feelings produce or colour thoughts? Although there is no real consensus on the matter, it is generally recognized that while some thoughts and feelings are apparently unrelated, many thoughts and feelings tend to be inseparable. It also has to be recognized that thoughts and feelings are produced as a result of perceptions or experiences of particular situations, and that thoughts and feelings can also contradict one another. For example, it is easy to like someone while simultaneously disapproving of them. The adage 'The heart hath its reasons of which reason knoweth not', also recognizes that what people do may not be wholly rational, but understandable when viewed from an emotional perspective.

Recent psychological thinking acknowledges that cognitions and emotions (psychological terms for thoughts and feelings) are closely related to one another. Imagine the last time you felt depressed, and try to recall what thoughts were going through your mind. Recall why you felt depressed at the time and think yourself back into the situation. Now ask yourself how you are feeling. It is likely that you are now feeling less buoyant than you were before you began the exercise.

Such a simple demonstration shows us that our thoughts can alter our feelings. But the opposite seems to be equally true: if we are feeling down, then we feel pessimistic about the future and imagine negative, rather than positive scenarios. Given that this relationship exists, how does it help us to understand the model of the world which our clients may have in their heads? In the first place, it shows us how a person's thoughts and feelings about themselves and their situation can form a schema through which the world is perceived, understood and acted upon.

SCHEMA THEORY

What is a schema? A schema is simply a mental framework which has a stable, internal structure. Because of its stable structure, a schema makes order out of a disordered set of experiences. A schema relating to how one feels about oneself now is what other people have referred to as the 'self-concept'. A schema relating to one's past and possibly future is what other people might call a 'life-script'. Schemas are simply a summary of one's dispositions, behaviour, attiudes, interests and so on, and they function to direct our attention to certain events, and to organize the ways in which we respond to these events (Fiske and Taylor, 1991).

Another important property of a schema is that the whole of it can be activated by any one part of it. For example, suppose we as rehabilitation workers go down to the supermarket. Immediately our attention is captured by someone using a white cane. The person we are with has noticed nothing, but we are already wondering whether we can be of any assistance to the individual. We find ourselves watching their mobility; we wonder who trained them; we think they could benefit from more training; we introduce ourselves to them or avoid them because we know them only too well. Our schema of our professional selves has been triggered by the stimulus of seeing a blind person, and we mentally swing into action.

Let us apply schema theory to a blind person's experience. Imagine that a cane user undertakes a new journey after having studied a tactile map of the area. He takes a wrong turn and spends some time figuring out where he might be. He hears approaching footsteps and asks a passer-by to direct him to his destination. The passer-by grabs him by the arm, and insists on taking him there. On leaving him, he tells him that blind people should not be walking about on their own as this is a dangerous area to be in. Into the traveller's mind flood images of incompetence, lack of sound judgment, embarrassment, humiliation, anger and resentment. The schema of the stereotype of the blind person has been triggered.

In our dealings with our clients we must be careful that we never act in such a way as to trigger such a schema. This is easier said than done, and I have personally witnessed many instances of O & M teachers unthinkingly placing blind people in dependent roles in social situations, usually by insisting on taking them by sighted guide when they do not require it, thereby triggering feelings of resentment which spoil further interactions with sighted people, at least for a short while until feelings have cooled off.

It is important to recognize that, once activated, a schema can direct attention to certain aspects of situations, that it can aid or prevent access to information stored in memory, and that it can organize automatic responses to situations. So that the blind person in the above example might become over-sensitive to neutral information which they interpret as further evidence for the truth of a negative stereotype, or they may give off signs of hostility which then cause others to avoid them. This avoidance, in turn, is interpreted as even further evidence for the validity of the stereotype. An activated negative schema can therefore produce feedback which causes feelings to spiral downwards into despair in the same way as an activated positive one can produce feedback resulting in euphoria.

Schema theory helps us to understand emotions such as depression and anxiety which characterize the initial reactions to loss of sight. The work of Beck (1989) has shown how depression is associated with schemata concerned with loss, together with negative aspects of the self, the world and the future. Beck's work shows how thoughts and feelings are closely linked, and his depressive schema involves a triad of cognitions, illustrated in Figure 3.1.

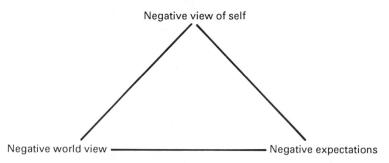

Negative view of self

Negative world view ——————————— Negative expectations

Figure 3.1 Beck's cognitive triad.

It has been shown that cognitive therapy, during which negative self attributes are confronted and gradually replaced by more positive ones, can alleviate chronic depressive states (Robertson and Brown, 1992), and attributional retraining can also help to change a depressed person's views about himself as small successes are emphasized and failures reconstrued in a more positive way (Weiner, 1979). Instead of regarding failure as a personal disaster, it should be considered as feedback indicating the need to improve performance on the next occasion. This leads to a constructive analysis of what might help improve matters, rather than generating further feelings of incompetence.

Recent research carried out at the Blind Mobility Research Unit at the University of Nottingham has identified a similar schema of thoughts and feelings in people who have just recently lost their sight (Dodds *et al.*, 1991c). Those clients who exhibit signs of depression are also highly anxious; have low self-esteem; have an external locus of control; believe they will fail at new tasks; hold negative attitudes towards blind people, and do not accept their own sight loss. If they are down on any one of those factors, then they are down on all the others as well, which suggests that the factors comprise inter-relating elements of a single structure which may be called adjustment.

In common with Beck, the view taken here is that by acting in such a way as to change each element of the structure, the rehabilitator can ensure that the whole structure undergoes a progressive change until it becomes replaced by a new one through which the individual interacts with the outside world and construes the self. This new structure has properties which were absent in the previous one, namely positive cognitions and emotions which produce behaviours which have satisfactory outcomes. These latter feed back to maintain the positive scheme. So how does the rehabilitator go about this task of restructuring their client's mental life in the absence of a psychologist?

In the first place, you do not subscribe to a negative stereotype of a blind person because you have seen for yourself just what people can do for themselves given the right sort of support and training. In the second place, you realize the need for the person to acquire some basic independence skills as well as having the ability to give these to the client. You also recognize that the ultimate aim of teaching independent living skills is to make the client feel that life is worth living again; to feel effective as a member of society; to be in control rather than being dependent upon other people, and to give back a sense of self esteem which has got lost along the way.

In order to be able to change your client's mental model of himself into one which more approximates yours, it is necessary to have a comprehensive understanding of him on a number of levels, ranging from the physiological, through the psychological, to the social. Before going on to address the nuts and bolts of delivering rehabilitation skills, we will first of all take a look at a number of factors which are of crucial relevance to the understanding of what your client may or may not be able to do. Once these have been addressed, we will be in a better position to put into practice the teaching methods suggested later in the book in Chapter 8.

4

Perception as information-processing

In order to behave appropriately in the environment the individual needs to have information about its layout. The environment is best thought of as an arrangement of surfaces, one lying in a horizontal plane, the other two lying at some angle in relation to one another in the vertical plane. In mobility, for example, the task of the traveller is to maintain contact with the horizontal surface while avoiding contact with the vertical ones. Jansson (1985) has analysed the task of mobility into walking towards, walking along and walking around. To this one needs to add *walking upon*, and it is the business of safely walking upon surfaces which presents the blind traveller with the greatest challenge.

When we consider the situation, the reason for this is obvious: horizontal surfaces are discontinuous much of the time. There are up-kerbs, down-kerbs and steps to contend with as we move forwards, and we need to be able to respond in time to these surface changes if we are to avoid an accident. Before going on to examine the nature of blind mobility, let us first of all take a look at how visually controlled movement depends upon the ability to obtain the information necessary for safe travel.

In the first book, *Mobility Training for Visually Handicapped People* (Dodds, 1988a), the two concepts of the optic array and perceptual invariance were introduced in order to account for sighted and non-sighted locomotion alike. These concepts are admittedly difficult to grasp, and in the space available they received only a relatively cursory treatment. In this chapter we shall have the opportunity of taking a look at them at a more leisurely pace, and in greater detail.

THE OPTIC ARRAY AND THE CONCEPT
OF INVARIANCE

The optic array is a term introduced by Gibson (1966) in order to account for how accurate visual perception of the environment is possible. Gibson single-handedly created a whole discipline known as 'ecological optics', which is concerned not so much with how light rays are bent by lenses (the sort of thing opticians and optometrists study), but with how light is structured by the environment and how this structure can be detected by the visual system to control our behaviour appropriately.

Gibson initially studied pilots taking off and landing aircraft at night, where the only information comes from rows of landing lights standing out as point sources of light against a black background. As the aircraft approaches them, they appear to stream outwards from their vanishing points. From this information, pilots are able to direct the aircraft, taking off and landing at speeds many times faster than walking. Gibson set himself the task of trying to explain how this was possible, given the drastically reduced information available to the eye.

He came to the conclusion that it was the movement of the points of light upon the retina which provided the brain with the information it needed to control the aircraft, but existing theories of perception could not explain how this was possible. He therefore set himself the task of looking for regularities in the ways in which the points of light moved. He discovered that there were several ways in which the movement was invariantly related to the situation responsible for producing it. For example, if the plane was to land on the runway, the pilot had to move the controls to ensure that the centre of the expansion pattern was on the point of the runway on which he wanted to land. Figure 4.1 shows this situation. If however, the centre of the expansion pattern was placed somewhere else, for example on the horizon, then that would be where the plane was pointing, as can be seen from Figure 4.2.

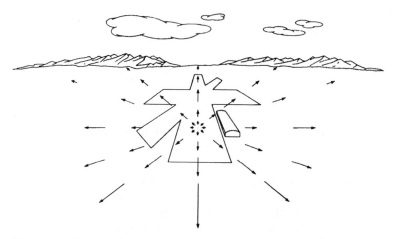

Figure 4.1 Centre of expansion pattern on landing area of runway.

Figure 4.2 Centre of expansion pattern on horizon.

When looking at walking, the situation is identical. The point one is walking towards is the centre of the optical expansion pattern, and any veering from the trajectory is corrected by detecting when this expansion pattern goes off centre. The changes in the optic array which specify that something is going to hit us are the same, only they take place in a portion of the visual field rather than all over it. Young babies show defensive arm movements when presented with a looming stimulus whose expansion pattern is symmetrical about the centre, but they do not show the same defensive behaviour when the expansion pattern of the stimulus is asymmetrical about the centre (Bower, Broughton and Moore, 1970). A central, symmetrical pattern specifies something on a hit path; a central, asymmetrical pattern specifies something on a miss path, and the visual system appears to be attuned to this at an early age.

When there is plenty of light available, the surfaces of the environment reflect and scatter light falling on them. So that instead of having perhaps 100 landing lights marking out a runway at night, there are potentially billions of light rays being reflected from facets of surfaces during daylight. This is what Gibson calls the optic array, and it can be thought of as form-ing an invisible, three-dimensional cobweb, through which we move. It is invisible because each ray of light carries no infor-mation on its own, only energy, but the array as a whole carries information specific to the environment when viewed from a particular location within it.

Gibson realized that perception consists of extracting infor-mation, whereas sensation merely registers the presence or absence of a stimulus of a particular intensity and duration. Light consists of little packets of energy known as photons, and when a photon strikes a retinal receptor, it releases its energy. Because of the law of conservation of energy, this energy has to go somewhere, and in the case of the receptor, it is changed into a tiny electrical impulse which combines with others and travels up the optic nerve to the brain. However, considering light as energy does not help us to understand perception: in order to do that, we need to think about the information contained in the light reflected from the environment.

Let us go back to surfaces for a moment, because they play a vital role in structuring reflected light. Most surfaces differ from one another in their composition, and this is particularly true of the man-made environment. Because of their different composition, surfaces absorb, reflect and scatter light waves in different ways. Some surfaces are shiny, others less so, and others again appear quite rough. Surfaces differ in colour, depending upon the selective absorption of wavelengths of light. All of these factors contribute to the perception of discontinuities between surfaces, and enable the eye to pick up that they are distinct from one another.

As we move through the environment, we create regular transformations or changes in the pattern of stimulation on our retinas. Because textural elements move together within a surface but move apart from one another between surfaces, the layout of the visual world is revealed. Surfaces move in front of others, hiding them; then they move out of the way, revealing the original surfaces once again. These movements, known as occlusions (coverings) at a leading edge; disocclusions (uncoverings) at a trailing edge, and wipings or shearings at adjacent edges, reveal the relationship of surfaces to one another. An occlusion or a disocclusion of one surface by another indicates a surface's relationship to other surfaces, effectively revealing depth. In real life, several occlusions and disocclusions may take place simultaneously, specifying a number of surfaces laid out relative to one another.

As we walk through the environment, these transformations in the optic array reveal to the eye and brain the layout of the environment. We produce these transformations as a result of our own movements and, without them, perception would be unreliable. The visual illusions which psychologists are so fond of demonstrating are invariably produced because of insufficient information which would disambiguate a perception. Static illusions abound, but few dynamic ones exist. Those which do tend to be the result of artificial environments with which our perceptual systems have not evolved to deal, or very rarely occurring events which have little or no evolutionary consequence, and examples of these have been given previously (Dodds, 1988a).

Two common real-world illusions are worth mentioning, because they both depend upon the same principle. The first is when we are sitting in a railway carriage and the train next to us pulls out. We immediately perceive that we are moving off in the opposite direction. Similarly, in a car-wash, we might panic for a moment when we perceive our car to be moving forwards, and stab at the brake pedal, when all that is happening is that the wash rollers are advancing towards us. These instances of what is called induced motion arise because the visual system relies on a frame of reference which in most situations is static. Any movement of the whole frame of reference usually specifies our own movement, but in those artificial conditions it is the frame of reference which is moving, and when this occurs our brains are fooled.

Perceptual systems, whether they be visual, auditory or tactile, depend upon the same principles; receptor surfaces need to be stimulated over time in order for the brain to extract the information. One of the basic requirements of any stimulus is that it has an onset, a duration and an offset, and this is true for all sensory modalities. The eye, even when it appears to be at rest, is in constant movement due to tremor. This is necessary for vision to take place at all, and images stabilized on the retina disappear altogether within a few seconds (Pritchard, 1958). The same is true for the skin: if stimuli are presented to it they cease to be felt if they remain static. The ears, because of the way that sounds come and go in the environment, similarly receive information over time, so that change over time is a very basic perceptual requirement.

When we turn to the non-visual control of locomotion, we are at once struck by the poverty of information available to the traveller. Gone is the optic flow which can specify the direction of travel, so that veering can be expected. Gone too are the occlusions and disocclusions which specify changes in surfaces, so that we can expect the person to trip and fall when surface changes occur beneath his feet. Gone are the expanding patterns produced by approaching obstacles, so that we can expect the person to collide with objects in his path. Without advance warning of changes in the environment movement becomes risky and anxiety-provoking. With suitable training, provision of a long cane virtually at a stroke makes mobility possible. How does it come to afford the apparent ease of movement which it does?

KINAESTHETIC INVARIANCE

In the first place, it gives the traveller a small increase in his preview of the environment. Although this amounts to only two paces, this is sufficient to enable him to walk at normal speeds with the confidence of being able to stop if the cane encounters an obstacle. But where is the invariance which the brain needs to work on? If we think about the way in which the client is taught to use the cane we can understand the importance of correct technique in its relation to invariance.

With the arm held so that the hand is positioned in the midline, the cane is moved repeatedly from side to side with wrist action only. At each end-point in the cane's arc, the cane-tip touches the ground, producing an invariant angle between the hand and the arm provided that the surface of the ground does not change its level or the arm does not change its position. With extensive practice, the angle of the wrist becomes familiar, and any changes in this angle can be immediately detected. The sense has been traditionally known as kinaesthesis (*kinein* – to move; *aethanesthai* – to perceive). Although invariance is not traditionally seen to be a property of the kinaesthetic sense, the fixed arm technique produces an invariant relationship between wrist angle and surface height.

When the surface changes its level, for example at a down-kerb, the angle at the wrist immediately increases and the user knows that the height of the surface ahead of him has changed. Similarly, the position of surfaces to the left and right are signalled by the cane tip stopping short of a full arc. The wrist is unable to travel to its intended position, and the user knows that he must veer to the left or to the right in order to avoid a collision. These relaitonships are invariant: an increase in wrist angle means a drop in the level of the surface; a reduction in wrist angle indicates a rise in the level of the surface. Poor cane use in which the arm is allowed to flex at the elbow or the shoulder leads to loss of invariance and hence to unreliable travel, so that good cane technique is essential if your client is to develop any confidence in the system.

AUDITORY INVARIANCE

The idea of invariance also helps us to understand how the blind traveller is able to use sounds to control his walking. Next to tactile information, auditory information is the most important, and a bonus of the touch technique for the long cane is that the traveller continually produces tapping sounds with his cane tip. These self-generated sounds enable him to detect the presence of obstacles by means of echo-location. Echo-location is itself a form of invariance detection, and it is possible because of two factors. The first is the constant speed of sound; the second is the relatively constant speed of walking. Although changes in each of those factors do occur in practice, they are usually so small as to be of academic interest only.

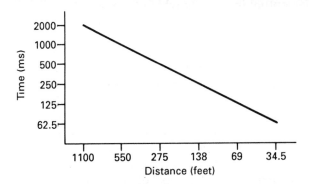

Figure 4.3 Invariant relationship between time and distance for a sound travelling from source to reflecting surface, and back again.

Figure 4.3 illustrates the invariant relationship between time and distance for a sound travelling from its source to a reflecting surface, and back again. The further the sound is from the surface, the longer it takes to return to its point of origin; the closer it is to the surface, the shorter is the time taken to return. This relationship is linear or invariant with respect to distance, so that the time taken by the sound to return to its origin specifies the distance of the reflecting surface. If the traveller maintains an invariant rate of progress, the rate at which the sound changes in its time to return to its origin is also constant, so that the rate of change in the time of the sound to return to its origin specifies time to collision. Those of you who may be mathematically inclined will recognize that this represents a second-order invariant produced by differentiating the slope of the line with respect to distance.

Another aspect of sounds is that they bear a unique relationship to the physical situation which produces them. This is because, like light, sound waves are structured by the environment. This structure can be a direct result of the way in which the sound is produced, for example by means of wind or friction between two surfaces. We can all tell the difference between a trumpet and a cello because the sound quality gives away the method by which the sound was produced. Of course, such judgements may require lengthy experience, and they are not to be regarded in the same way as perceptual invariants which leap out at us, but it goes to show how much perceptual learning is possible given sufficient practice.

By repeatedly walking about through the environment the blind traveller can learn that there are regularities in the ways in which sounds behave. In addition to being specified by the reflection of self-generated sounds, objects, if they are sufficiently large, can be specified by the fact that they occlude distant, ambient sounds. Bus-shelters and the like can therefore be observed as they are passed, first of all, by means of sound-shadowing and, second, by means of echo-location. A good auditory analogue of the visual disocclusion of surfaces is when a building line is passed, revealing the distant sounds which were previously masked by it. This can warn the traveller of an approaching turn or down-kerb to be encountered, and travellers with a good auditory awareness can use such sound cues to enable them to anticipate a corner without having to walk as far as the down-kerb.

PERCEPTUAL REDUNDANCY

The term 'redundancy' is one which is familiar to research psychologists (literally as well as scientifically!), but its special meaning may not be understood generally. Redundancy exists when something is over-specified in terms of the information available. For example, as the eye moves through the optic array, changes occur all over the retina simultaneously. These changes are consistent with one another, so that we need to be aware only of one or two of the thousands which are taking place. We do not sample every single possible part of visual space as we move through it because it would take us all day to do this before being confident of taking a single step. Instead, because the information is replicated over and over again, we simply take the occasional sample, pausing only now and again to scrutinize something more closely.

By contrast, the auditory world is seriously lacking in redundancy, so that auditory information arrives at our ears only intermittently, and part of the job of the blind traveller is to strain his ears in the hope of catching some sound which will inform him of where he is on his route. Whereas the visual world continually proclaims itself to our eyes, the auditory world is largely silent, save for the occasional sound revealing the presence of some feature of the environment. Leonard (1970) emphasized how visually guided locomotion might be unique in this respect, and how this may place limits on what can be achieved in blind mobility.

In his book, Hull (1990) makes mention of how much more he is aware of the environment when it is raining. Each surface structures the sound of the rain differently, so that when the world is irradiated with the sound of the rain falling, the surfaces which make it up are revealed. Before, when they were silent, the situation could be likened to the auditory equivalent of being invisible to the eyes. I recall a similar instance when I accompanied a blind person to a firework display. As the rockets exploded in a burst, so the sounds echoed off the buildings around us. My friend observed that he had not 'seen' these buildings for 20 years, but now he could while the rockets were going off. Whether or not visual impressions were automatically triggered from visual memory is an open question, but it is undeniable that if an 'acoustic array' could be created, the blind person would have a conscious awareness of the environment which he otherwise lacks. This principle, whether stated or implicit, underlies the development of all ultrasonic mobility devices.

SUPPLEMENTING AUDITORY INFORMATION

It has been generally recognized that to present additional information about the environment to the blind traveller might be one means of improving his travel and reducing the stress he experiences. Without the luxury of redundancy, the traveller has to work hard to get the information he needs, and very often, when he gets it, it comes all at once, effectively swamping his brain. This means that he cannot process it in time to make the best decision or to choose the most appropriate behaviour, producing what we would call stress, in that demands are being placed upon him which he cannot meet, given his current resources. This is one of the defining features of stress, which we shall consider more fully in Chapter 8.

The Sonic Torch

In an attempt to provide the traveller with information in advance of it being required, a number of electronic devices have been invented over the last 25 years or so. The earliest of these devices was the Sonic Torch, invented by Professor Leslie Kay. Kay's invention utilized ultrasound and the principle of invariance outlined earlier. The device consists of a pair of electronic transducers, one emitting ultrasonic pulses mounted on top of another which received any sound reflected back from objects in its path. The Sonic Torch is illustrated in Figure 4.4.

Figure 4.4 The Sonic Torch.

The upper transducer converts electrical energy into pulses of ultrasound which sweep from 90kHz down to 45kHz three times every second. When the beam of sound strikes an object in front of the device, some of that sound is reflected back towards the device where it is received by the lower transducer. Because the sound frequency sweeps down during each pulse, the frequency of the sound being emitted at the time when the echo is received will be less than that at the beginning of the pulse. The device mixes the incoming echo signal with the emitting signal, and converts the resulting frequency into an audible signal which the user's ears can pick up. Such a system is known as frequency modulation, or FM, as is used in radio transmission.

Using the Sonic Torch, the traveller hears an audible tone which decreases in frequency the closer the device is to a target. By extracting the second-order invariant, the user can predict time to collision. Useful as one might imagine such a device to be, an evaluation of it carried out at the time (Leonard, 1970) found that few blind people could make use of the device. Those who could appeared to be filtering out a lot of additional information which the device provided, such as textural information, and it was concluded that ultrasonic devices should have a simpler display if they were to be understood by the average traveller.

The Sonicguide

In spite of the conclusions reached by Leonard, Kay further developed the Sonic Torch to make it more compatible with the mechanisms of the brain involved in normal auditory perception. In addition, he recognized that the Sonic Torch had to be scanned from side to side during travel, thereby creating the additional task of keeping track of where it was pointing. This made it difficult to perceive exactly where the objects lay in relation to the device as the user moved through the environment. Whereas the Sonic Torch may be thought of as an obstacle detector, what Kay really wanted to produce was an environmental sensor.

Kay's solution to these problems represented a *tour de force* at the time, resulting in a device known as the Sonicguide, which is illustrated in Figure 4.5. Whereas the Sonic Torch

Figure 4.5 The Sonicguide.

has only one receiver, the Sonicguide has two. Between the two receivers lies a transmitter which emits pulses of ultrasound. Inconspicuously mounted on a spectacle frame, the Sonicguide provides the wearer with true stereophonic information about the environment. This is made possible by the use of varying intensities of sound being presented to each ear, depending upon the position of the object. When the object lies to the left, the volume of the sound in the left ear is greater than that in the right. When the object occupies a central position, the volume of the sound in each ear is the same. When the object lies to the right, the volume of the sound in the right ear is greater than that in the left. This situation is identical to that which would be obtained in the case of sound-making objects in those positions.

Although objective evaluations of the Sonicguide have not managed to show significant changes in the behaviour of travellers using the device, this does not mean that the device does not benefit the user. People who volunteer for evaluations are usually highly competent long-cane travellers, and their mobility is probably as good as it will ever be. This is why evaluations which look only at their moment-to-moment mobility performance may be unable to demonstrate the benefits of the device. However, there may be a genuine improvement in the users' perception of the environment which can increase their confidence and make their travel more relaxed. If this should be the case, evaluative procedures need to take these factors into account.

The Sonic Pathfinder

Following Leonard's conclusions on the Sonic Torch, Tony Heyes of the Blind Mobility Research Unit developed a small, hand-held device known as the Nottingham Obstacle Detector (NOD). Although the NOD never became commercially viable, it showed that a simple display could be used to good advantage without the need for extensive training, and some of its features were retained in a new device known as the Sonic Pathfinder (Heyes, 1984). The Pathfinder utilizes a microprocessor which enables it to do a number of things depending on the environmental circumstances and the user's behaviour (Figure 4.6).

Unlike the Sonicguide, which has a true stereophonic signal, that of the Pathfinder divides space up into three zones: a left zone, a central zone and a right zone. Whereas the Sonicguide displays space simultaneously, the Pathfinder displays each of these three zones in turn over a short space of time, looking left, then centre, then right, then centre, and so on. The distance of an object within each zone is represented by the musical scale developed for the NOD. If an obstacle presents itself on a collision path, the two side channels are silenced, and the musical scale is presented at twice the repetition rate to both ears simultaneously, thus serving to capture attention and to warn the user of a potential collision.

Figure 4.6 The Sonic Pathfinder.

As a result of an evaluation of an earlier prototype (Dodds, Clark-Carter and Howarth, 1984), it was found that the device produced more information than the user could cope with in cluttered environments, and a modification was made to ensure that its range was reduced under such conditions. The evaluation further showed that the Pathfinder can make the user aware of the presence of shorelines which he is then able to follow by means of keeping the tone in the appropriate ear constant; that it can improve walking speed after sufficient practice; and that these benefits can be obtained only at the slight expense of being less aware of certain environmental sounds. Further developments included the ability of the device to alter its range depending upon the user's walking speed, extending its degree of preview as the user speeds up. The resulting device is therefore very flexible, minor changes in the software enabling it to be bespoke to the user's requirements.

One difficulty with all new devices is that no-one knows in advance just how much training is required. Although the Pathfinder utilizes the same musical scale as the Nottingham Obstacle Detector, the fact that it displays the scale to both ears in quick succession leads to initial confusion if a number of targets are present simultaneously. Its inventor claims that it can be mastered within two days with good training (personal communication), but research has yet to determine what factors are involved in 'good training'.

The Wheelchair Pathfinder

This is a device aimed at the visually impaired user who is confined to a wheelchair, and two versions are available. The first, uses ultrasound to detect vertical surfaces and obstacles to the side of the traveller. The second has the addition of a laser beam which can detect drops ahead, and it thereby gets round a number of problems from which ultrasonic devices suffer. The manufacturers claim that it can detect obstacles ahead as far away as eight feet; that it can detect surfaces on each side at twelve inches, and that it can detect drops when the wheelchair is within four feet of a step or kerb. Such a range of features makes it a highly attractive aid for thse who are unable to walk (Figure 4.7).

The display consists of various tones, each of which is assigned to one of its three functions. Objects ahead trigger an intermittent bleeping sound; objects to the side trigger one

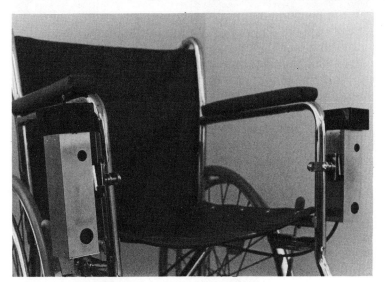

Figure 4.7 The Wheelchair Pathfinder.

of two continuous tones, and drops ahead trigger a low-pitched tone. The device can be used to find a clear path simply by means of the user turning his wheelchair until the device falls silent. Alternatively, a landmark can be reached by means of keeping the beeping signal directly ahead of the chair.

For a client who has a unilateral spatial neglect (see Chapter 5) the Side Alert represents a modification of the device. The presence of an obstacle is signalled by both an audio alarm and a flashing liquid electronic display (LED). Upon receiving the signal, the user visually scans into the area of neglect. The device can be considered to be a training device, or in the case of a client who fails to learn to scan into the neglected side upon receipt of the alarm signal, a device to be worn continuously.

The Mowat Sensor

Another device which was developed on the basis of the Sonic Torch is the Mowat Sensor (Figure 4.8). Employing pulsed

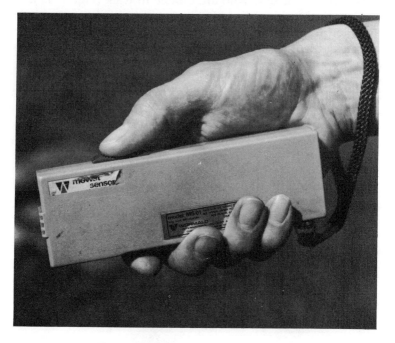

Figure 4.8 The Mowat Sensor.

ultrasound, it utilizes a vibratory display which can be switched to one of two ranges of operating distance: up to one metre or up to four metres. These ranges represent appropriate distances for indoor and outdoor usage, respectively. In the absence of a target, the device is silent, and it responds only to the nearest object if there are several in its path at once. The display has an invariant relationship with the distance at which an object is situated from it, in common with all devices employing ultrasound.

When the device is aimed at an object which is close at hand, it vibrates rapidly: when it is pointed at an object farther away, it throbs slowly in the hand. Additionally, the device has provision for an ear-piece which delivers a tone whose frequency varies inversely with the distance from an object. These invariant relationships allow the user to predict quite accurately the time to collision, although they do not permit absolute distance judgements to be made. However, time to collision information is very useful, and the device continues to sell in small but steady numbers.

The Polaron

A recently developed ultrasonic mobility aid has arisen from the technology surrounding auto-focus cameras. The Polaron is a hand-held or chest-mounted device which can detect objects within four, eight or 16 feet (Figure 4.9). The display consists either of a tone or a vibration, and in this respect the device resembles the Mowat Sensor. However, in the chest-mounted mode, a miniaturized vibrator mounted in the strap displays range information to the back of the neck. As in the Mowat, the frequency of the vibration and the tone increase as the device approaches an object. One feature of the Polaron is that it can be mounted on a wheelchair. In fact, it is possible to mount two of the devices on a wheelchair, one facing left and the other right. This enables the user to shoreline on either side of a corridor, thereby maintaining a straight line of travel.

The Laser Cane

The devices so far described utilize ultrasound to interrogate the environment, producing an acoustic equivalent of the

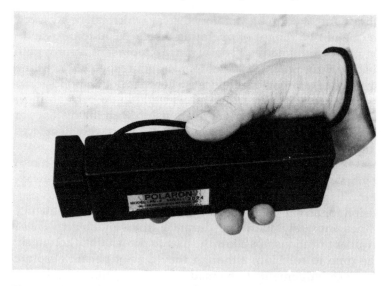

Figure 4.9 The Polaron.

optic array. The environment structures this energy, producing information for the user where before there was none. As we shall see later, there are unsurmountable drawbacks to devices which depend upon ultrasound, and the Laser Cane represents an alternative approach to the problem of providing additional environmental information to the user.

The electronics of the device are incorporated into a long cane, and this is useful in that it leaves the user's other hand free to carry something, unlike the other hand-held devices which tie up the user's free hand. The device emits pulses of low-powered laser light in the infra-red region of the spectrum which is invisible to the human eye. Light is sent out in three directions: up, ahead and down, and three receivers look in those directions in order to catch any reflected light from objects in their path. The output of the device consists of both tactile and audible signals, and each receiver has a unique output. This enables the user to tell where the object lies, or whether there is a drop or a rise in a kerb edge (Figure 4.10). A distinct advantage of the Laser Cane is that it can still serve perfectly well as a long cane even if the battery should run down.

In relation to other devices which provide more than just information about single objects lying in their path, the Laser Cane is a serious contender both in terms of cost and benefit.

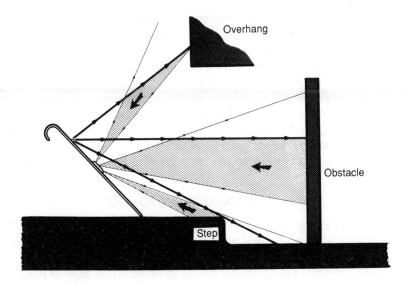

Figure 4.10 The Laser Cane.

COST/BENEFIT RATIOS

Cost/benefit ratios are important factors when choosing a device, and the Laser Cane, which retails for around £2 500, compares favourably with the cost of the Sonicguide, which appears to be virtually unobtainable now. Hand-held obstacle detectors such as the Mowat and the Polaron cost £450 and £550 respectively, and the cost of the Sonic Pathfinder is around £1 000. The Wheel-chair Pathfinder is available in two versions: the first, which lacks the laser, costs £1 500, and the second, which includes it, sells at £2 200. By explaining to your client what devices can and cannot do you can help him make a sensible decision, and evaluations conducted by impartial authorities are invaluable in assisting you.

EVALUATION

To date, no-one has conducted an objective evaluation of all the devices whch are available. This is partly because not all devices purport to do the same thing, and because certain devices are in limited supply (the Sonicguide is currently unavailable in the UK). However, Blasch, Long and Griffin-Shirley (1989) carried out a follow-up evaluation of usage of electronic travel aids (ETAs) in the United States. They found that a high percentage of users reported big differences in their ability to avoid obstacles at body and head level; to assess distance and direction of objects; to avoid pedestrians in a crowd and to locate the door of a building.

The authors concluded that out of the four ETAs investigated, the Laser Cane seemed to be the most commonly used on a regular basis. As a result of asking users what modifications they would like to have made, suggestions for an even better device are being taken on board by the manufacturers. This is a good example of collaboration between device manufacturers, designers and psychologists, which can only be of ultimate benefit to the user group.

INSURMOUNTABLE DRAWBACKS

Before leaving the area of supplementary information, it is worth pointing out that all ultrasonic devices suffer from an inability to provide the traveller with the necessary and sufficient information which he needs in order to be able to plan the next step, something which the cane does admirably. Not only is it important to know if there is an obstacle ahead, it is absolutely vital to safe and smooth mobility to know whether or not the surface of the ground is level.

Lest anyone underestimate the importance of this, it must be recognized that the planning of the next step, which takes place within half a second, depends crucially upon deciding whether that step should be a step straight ahead like the last one; a step to the right or to the left; or a step up or a step down. There are two reasons why ultrasonic devices cannot obtain the information necessary for the planning of a step.

The first is because the wavelength of ultrasound, short as it is in relation to audible sound, is still comparatively long with respect to the size of the particles in surfaces specified by light. This is known as the 'grain size' problem. It means that to all intents and purposes many surfaces are indistinguishable from one another, and surfaces lying closer together than the wavelength of the ultrasound do not appear to be separate. The occlusions and disocclusions, the wipings and shearings present in the optic array, have no counterpart in the acoustic array at the level of resolution required.

The second, even more serious, but equally insurmountable problem is that a surface which appears rough to the eye working on the optic array behaves like a mirror to the ear working on an ultrasonic acoustic array. This is again due to the 'grain size' of the environment with respect to ultrasound. If the sound is directed at an angle towards the surface, instead of being reflected back into the device, triggering a signal, it is reflected away from the device, producing no signal (Figure 4.11), so that the user perceives that there is a clear path ahead when in fact there may be a wall in front of him. Psychologists call this a false negative; that is to say the information says that nothing has changed when in fact it has.

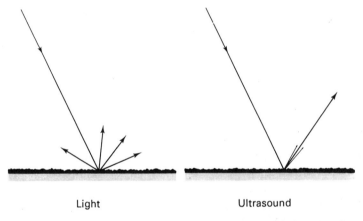

Light   Ultrasound

Figure 4.11 The reflective characteristics of light and ultrasound.

The Laser Cane is subject to a similar criticism, although to a lesser degree. On a wet day, surfaces reflect light energy away from the device, causing it to signal the presence of a drop. This means that although in actual fact it is safe to proceed, the user perceives that he needs to stop before taking a step down. Psychologists call this a false positive, that is to say the information says that something has changed when in fact it has not. False negatives and positives detract from the reliability of devices and can cause the user to lose confidence them. When training a client in their use, this should be pointed out, and the client should be taught to rely on the information coming through the cane tip whenever there is any doubt.

With hindsight, it is sad to observe that many problems in the use of these devices could have been anticipated, had the right people been consulted, as there is a large body of knowledge on perception and learning in existence. Jansson (1985) points out that non-engineering people such as psychologists are included in the discussions on aid development relatively late in the process, and urges an interaction between engineering and perception–action experts at an early stage. It is hoped that this can be achieved in future research. But one has to recognize that even the best electronic device can be regarded only as a secondary travel aid to a cane or a dog, and this situation is likely to obtain for the next 20 years or so, when research into moving robots may well change the picture.

RECENT DEVELOPMENTS

Years of effort by a number of individuals have failed to produce the technological revolution of mobility that had been dreamed of 30 years ago. However, recent applications of high technology are beginning to have a greater impact on modifying the environment through which the traveller moves, rather than on the traveller who moves through that environment. The REACT Project, funded by the Royal National Institute for the Blind, utilizes electronic transmission of coded information which is placed on appropriate aspects of the environment such as pillar-boxes or Pelican crossings, and which is picked up by means of an electronic sensing device carried by the user.

In a similar vein, recent research carried out by the Guide Dogs for the Blind Association in Britain has resulted in the production of a prototype Orientation Assistance Device (OAD). Operating on a similar principle to that of the REACT system, the OAD consists of a transmitter mounted on an appropriate piece of street furniture, whose signal can be picked up by the traveller. This signal can trigger a pre-recorded, spoken message which enables the traveller to make the correct decision upon reaching a down-kerb, thereby relieving him of the task of memorizing huge amounts of information on long routes. Such approaches to improving orientation and mobility are likely to burgeon over the next decade as the components required for such technology become cheaply mass-produced for other purposes such as surveillance.

In this chapter we have covered the basic ground of information extraction, whether this involves the eyes, the ears or the hand. In each perceptual mode the principle remains the same: invariant relationships are extracted from changes in stimulation of the sense organs over time. This is possible because the brain is able to process complex changes in stimulation arising out of our own movements to tell us about the environment and our relationship to it. Blind mobility is possible because of this, and although the eyes of sighted people may provide the most information for the brain to work on, other senses can provide sufficient invariance for the brain to get by when the eyes can no longer be relied upon to do so. The next chapter explains how this process can be impaired by damage to various parts of the brain.

5

The brain

Perception involves the active searching for and processing of information. Although we are traditionally regarded as possessing five separate senses, these senses are better thought of as information-processing systems sharing the same basic principles. In the last century, scientists believed that our brains were specialized into different areas which were responsible for different functions. To some extent they were right, and we now know a considerable amount about how specialized areas in the brain are responsible for processing different kinds of information.

However, some of the early ideas about brain specialization were downright fanciful, and quasi-sciences such as phrenology (the science of reading bumps on the head) developed. To the modern neuropsychologist, the idea that different parts of the brain are responsible for such personality traits as diverse as generosity or moral sense is ridiculous and the development of a sound understanding of neuropsychological functioning was impeded by unscientific speculations which took some time to become discredited.

Nowadays however, many of the brain's mysteries have been unravelled, and this knowledge helps us to form a coherent picture of a person's remaining abilities or deficits when they are unfortunate enough to have suffered some form of brain damage. The following sections look at the brain from a number of useful perspectives, beginning with the more primitive parts responsible for our basic life functions; then moving on to consider the newer, cortical parts of the brain, including the visual system, and finally to examine the role of other parts of the cortex which help to control intelligent behaviour.

SUBCORTICAL AREAS

First, let us take a brief look at the brain in fairly global terms. The surface of the brain is covered with the most recently evolved part known as the cortex. This can be seen in Figure 5.1, which also bears the names of the different parts of the cortex to which the reader will be referred later in this chapter. Beneath the cortex lie the oldest parts of the brain, parts which we share in common with the lower mammals.

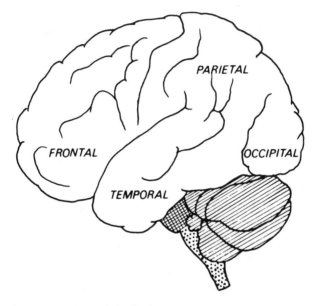

Figure 5.1 Main areas of the brain.

In evolutionary terms, the cortex of the brain represents its most recent development. Yet beneath it lie ancient parts of the brain. These structures are responsible for our basic instincts and the more primitive processes underlying learning, and without them we would not have survived for long enough to evolve a cortex at all. They still play a vital role in regulating our behaviour, although we are completely unaware of their existence when they are left intact to perform their various functions. When they are damaged, however, considerable deficits are likely to emerge, and it is important to understand the variety of ways in which

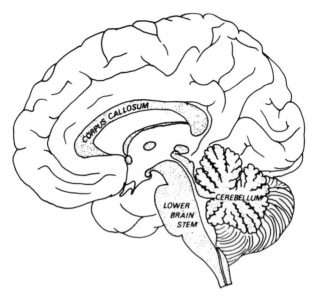

Figure 5.2 Areas of the brain responsible for regulating consciousness.

behaviour can be altered dramatically through the absence of malfunction of these subcortical areas.

Let us begin with the most basic psychological function, namely the state of consciousness. In our everyday lives we experience the gaining of consciousness called wakefulness, and its opposite, the loss of consciousness, which is called sleep. Our brains alternate between these two states which, as we have seen in Chapter 3, are linked to daylight and darkness. The parts of the brain responsible for regulating these states lie just above the top of the spinal cord, in the base of the brain, and are illustrated in Figure 5.2. They can be thought of as the activating part of the brain, getting the whole system into a state of readiness for action. Damage to these areas has disastrous consequences for the organism, producing coma.

Closely connected to the activating system lie the parts responsible for determining what sorts of activity need to be carried out in order for the organism to survive, such as feeding, fighting, fleeing and reproducing. Damage to these parts of the brain can produce such behaviour as over-eating and emotional states such as rage or uncontrollable weeping.

In addition, responsiveness to external stimulation is controlled by these areas, and lesions can affect the ability of the person to attend to external stimuli. The next chapter illustrates how seriously the learning process can be affected in a person with damage to these areas of the brain.

A third function associated with the midbrain is that of memory. Lesions in this area can seriously disrupt the client's ability to recall any new information, and tasks which have recently been completed are not recollected upon questioning. Even more puzzling is the client's inability to remember the names of people to whom he may be introduced, and the client may forever react to the instructor as if he has only just met her, even though they may have been working together on a daily basis.

THE VISUAL SYSTEM

It will be taken for granted that you are all sufficiently familiar with the detailed anatomy and physiology of the eye. However, the visual pathways to the brain and its associated machinery are likely to be less well known. The discipline which deals with such aspects of vision is known as neuro-ophthalmology, which represents a specialized part of an ophthalmologist's training. Yet, Rehabilitation Workers can benefit from some elementary knowledge of neuro-anatomy because it will help them to understand why a client may present a particular picture which, without such knowledge, might appear confusing.

Although the eye represents the first line in processing the information contained in the optic array, without an elaborately differentiated nervous system, perception would be an unsophisticated process, yielding only gross information to the organism. Perhaps this is best recognized by considering briefly visual systems which are much less complex than our own.

Our visual systems have evolved from more primitive ones over hundreds of thousands of years. Relatively simple organisms such as molluscs, for example, possess only rudimentary sense organs which signal the difference between light and dark. The receptor surface, which can loosely be thought of as corresponding to our retina, is only a slightly modified cup of skin with an associated nerve supply leading to an equally primitive 'brain'. By means of such a simple system, appropriate movements towards or away from light can be influenced as suits the life-style of the animal.

As we ascend the evolutionary tree this simple modification of the skin becomes progressively more specialized until an 'eye' can be differentiated from the surrounding tissue. By this stage the eye has become a dark chamber into which light enters via a lens or, in the case of insects, a number of lenses, each of which focuses the structured light reflected from the environment on to a sensitive receptor surface which carries nervous impulses to the brain. Such perceptual systems are capable of detecting changes in light levels, recognizing and identifying objects and registering changes in their movements. They also enable the animal to monitor changes in its own movements, whether these involve a part or the whole of the body.

Our own mammalian eyes are an impressive triumph of evolution, having developed in close conjunction with the hands. Indeed, some evolutionary theorists claim that the evolution of the hand and eye took place together: improvements in visual acuity providing an opportunity to develop finer movements and eventually structures in the hands and fingers; the resulting finer movements requiring the eye to develop even greater resolution than it had before. But however the eye evolved, it is the most powerful of the senses in that it can monitor changes in the environment at huge distances and in great detail over a very wide field.

HOW THE EYE AND BRAIN ARE CONNECTED

Although the mammalian eye has the superficial resemblance to a camera, this analogy grossly underestimates the complexity of visual perception and does not help us in the least in understanding why and how vision can be disturbed by events taking place at or beyond the retina in the neural machinery of the brain itself. Nor can the eye-as-camera analogy help us to understand how the various functions of visual perception are shared between different parts of the visual system, or how damage to one of the parts can selectively impair visual perception.

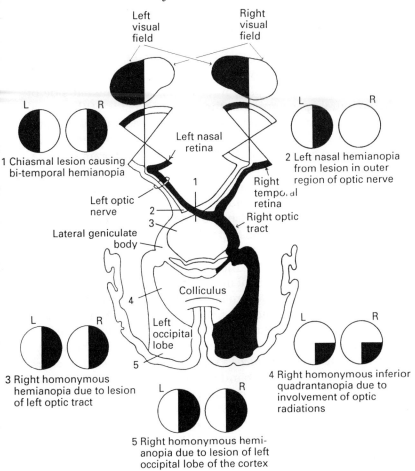

Figure 5.3 The human visual pathways (from above).

Figure 5.3 illustrates in simplified form the human visual pathways (imagine that you are above the head, looking down). The first point to note is that humans have two eyes, not just one. An immediate advantage of having two eyes is that if one becomes damaged we can still see almost as well with the remaining eye. Although true stereoscopic vision is lost, depth perception is only reduced, but not lost. This is due to the existence of perspective cues in the environment and motion parallax which tells the brain whether something lies behind or in front of something else.

The next point to note is that the spatial information from each retina is split into two at the optic chiasma (*chiasma* is simply Greek for a cross), information about the left side of behavioural space going to the right hand side of the visual cortex while information about the right side of behavioural space goes to the left side. This anatomical arrangement has important perceptual implications for localized brain damage, as shall be seen presently, because strokes frequently involve areas of the optic tract and may thereby interfere with the integrity of the visual field.

From Figure 5.3 it is also possible to see the effects on the visual fields of damage at particular locations in the visual pathways. A lesion at 1, where the optic nerves partly cross, results in a heteronymous (different sides) bi-temporal (on each side of the temples) hemianopia (half of the field is blind in each eye). This effectively means that the outer halves of visual space are missing), and this produces a form of tunnel vision. A lesion at 2 on the temporal side of the left optic nerve produces a left nasal (on the nose side) hemianopia in the left eye only. A lesion at 3 produces a right, homonymous (same sides) hemianopia (both eyes blind to the right side only). A lesion at 4 results in a right homonymous inferior (lower field) quadrantanopia (a quarter of the field is blind); and a lesion at 5 in the left occipital lobe of the visual cortex produces a right homonymnous hemianopia (both right sides of visual space are missing).

Do not panic if you cannot remember the cumbersome terminology used by neuro-ophthalmologists. The point of illustrating these defects is that they arise directly from injury to specific points in the visual pathway before the information from retina reaches the visual centres of the brain, or from damage to one of the visual centres itself. A person can have completely normal eyes and still suffer from considerable losses of vision as a result of damage further back in the system. But because of the layout of the visual centres themselves, damage to them produces its own unique pattern of visual loss.

In contrast to the perspective of Figure 5.3, Figure 5.4 looks at the brain from behind the head. Starting at the level of the retina, we know that receptor cells are divided into two

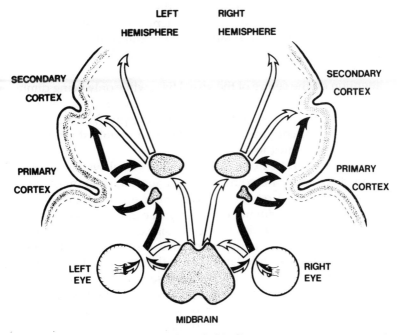

Figure 5.4 The human brain (from behind).

groups, the cones in the centre and the rods in the periphery, so that physiologically different cells are also anatomically distinct. As we move inwards, away from the retina and towards the brain, we see that the nervous pathways of these two different types of cell begin to diverge. The path of the information from the cones is through what is called the lateral, geniculate body; a kind of halfway house or relay station. On the other hand, the information from the rods passes through a structure known as the colliculus, which is located in the midbrain. Once the two sets of visual information have been partly processed at these two relay stations, they pass to the secondary association cortex where they are recombined, giving rise to a unified perception of the world.

THE TWO VISUAL SYSTEMS

What we understand now is that the eye is only one structure of several which processes information by means of what is effectively two visual systems; the central or focal visual system, and the peripheral or ambient visual system. Visual perception of fine detail takes place in the context of a complete spatial background which is itself poorly resolved until the macula is directed on to it. We consciously focus our attention on the centre of the visual field while only being dimly conscious of the surrounding ambient field. Yet we perceive the world as being continuous and sharply focused, even though it is discontinuous for our brains and only sharp inside a few degrees in the centre.

Evidence for the existence of the two visual systems comes from three separate sources; physiological, anatomical and behavioural, the first two of which have just been discussed. The third line of evidence comes from a combination of clinical and experimental studies where damage to the primary cortical analysers has been clearly established. Said to possess 'blindsight', individuals with damage to both of the occipital cortexes are unable to have the experience of seeing. Yet they can still carry out tasks such as being able to point to light sources at a level better than chance, to pick up objects although they cannot name them, and to avoid colliding with objects as they walk about.

The reason for this strange pattern of performance is due to the fact that the midbrain ambient system is left intact and can control behaviour appropriately, even though the cortical system can no longer give rise to the experience of sight. This phenomenon of blindsight is not to be confused with hysterical blindness, which is dealt with in the next chapter, and it is more common to find individuals with only one half of the visual field affected. Although it was fashionable for a time to discount blindsight as a combination of field defect and lowering of cognitive capacity, recent studies have reconfirmed its existence as a syndrome, albeit a rare one (Weiskrantz, 1990).

THE PRIMARY VISUAL ANALYSERS

Right at the back of the cortex lie the two primary visual processing stations, the 'twin peaks' of the brain. Referring back to Figure 5.3, we can see that a representation of half of each retina is laid out in each one. This means that the brain divides perceptual space into two in terms of information processing. However, we should not be misled into thinking of the visual information being 'projected' on to each visual cortex as a slide might be projected onto a screen. This would be falling back into the eye-as-camera metaphor which has been shown to

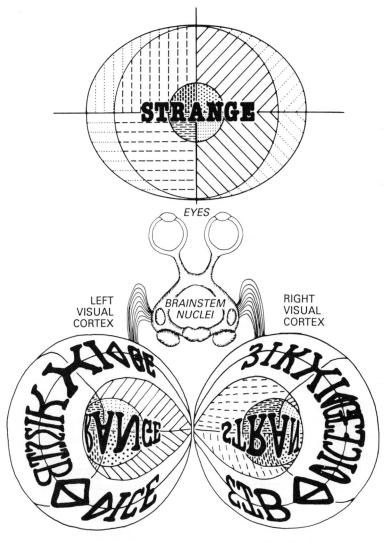

Figure 5.5 Projection of the retinal image onto the visual cortex.

be misleading. Figure 5.5 illustrates what a literal cortical projection of the nervous pathways would look like if we could see it. No little man in the head would be able to make much sense of the jumble which it appears to be, so that visual perception of the layout of the environment cannot be based on some sort of mechanism which literally 'scans' a picture on the surface of the brain.

Experiments in which electrical activity in the cortex is recorded have shown that the primary visual analysers contain cells which respond selectively to lines and edges of varying orientations. These cells are stacked in columns which extend some centimetres into the outer brain covering. Experiments in which electrical stimulation is applied to the brain have shown that when the primary visual analysers are stimulated, the patient sees flashes of light, spots of colour and the like. The results of these experiments tell us that objects are therefore first broken down into their primitive, constituent components for analysis before this information is passed to another part of the brain for yet further processing.

Damage to the central part of the occipital cortex, whether arising 'naturally' or experimentally results in scotomas, or holes, in the visual field which vary in area as function of the amount of cortex involved. Small, partial losses in the visual field are usually compensated for by eye movements, the exception being in the case of lesions in the right occipital cortex where a left-sided fixed hemianopia is often observed. This is never spontaneously compensated for and is most resistant to training.

THE SECONDARY VISUAL ZONES

Lying adjacent to the primary visual analysers are the secondary association areas of the brain. Again, experimental research combined with clinical evidence tells us that the information processed in the primary areas of the cortex is passed on to these secondary areas where it is combined with information arriving from the peripheral pathways. Remember, a proportion of this information was filtered off just after it left the retina; now it is recombined with the central information to give an impression of a complete and continuous visual field.

When the secondary visual analysers are stimulated electrically the results are completely different from those in which the primary analysers are stimulated. Patients will report seeing images of flowers, people, and so on, and sequences of events can be seen to occur over time, as in dreams. These findings illustrate clearly the role of the secondary visual analysers in synthesizing the information which the primary analyser has broken down into its constituent components.

Damage extending to the secondary occipital areas can produce a variety of visual problems known collectively as agnosias. Agnosias (*a* - without; *gnosos* - knowledge) are failures to recognize objects in the visual field. Agnosia is the inability to recognize an object, although people suffering from this condition can often use the object appropriately, even though they can not state its function.

Simultaneous agnosia consists of an inability to see two objects when they are placed side by side, although each object can be seen when presented individually. Alternatively, the individual may be unable to appreciate more than one feature of an object or picture at a time. The Soviet neuropsychologist Luria described such a case when he showed such a patient a picture of a pair of spectacles: 'He is confused and does not know what the picture represents. He starts to guess. "There is a circle ... and another circle ... and a stick ... and a cross-bar ... why, it must be a bicycle"' (Luria, 1973, p. 116).

Prosopagnosia is an inability to recognize faces, even although they are highly familiar, or to mistake objects for faces. Individuals suffering from this disorder are perfectly able to recognize a face as a face, but they are unable to say whose face it is. They may even be unable to recognize themselves in the mirror. Such cases are rare, and are usually accompanied by visual field defects such as a hemianopia, but Sacks (1985), *The Man Who Mistook His Wife For a Hat*, is well worth reading in order to understand how distressing such a condition can be. Those of you who wish to learn more about the visual system and the agnosias should consult Humphreys and Riddoch (1987), or Riddoch (1991), in the Disabled Living Foundation's distance learning pack.

Before leaving the visual processing areas of the brain we should consider the fact that seeing involves an active search for expected objects or features of objects, rather than just a simple and passive reception of visual information. Seeing involves making both eye and head movements in a co-ordinated and intelligent manner. We do not simply glance around us at random in the hope of seeing something of interest; our visual search is structured by our previous experiences in a more or less regular world, so that we look only at areas where we need to obtain information or where we expect change to occur.

The frontal lobes of the brain, which we shall examine in the next section, also play a part in visual perception. In the case of the individual with frontal lobe damage, the ability to make sense out of visual impressions is lost. Often we have to work out what it is we are looking at, particularly when we are presented with, say, a picture of a familiar object in an unusual orientation or at a scale we are unaccustomed to. Patients with frontal lobe damage often misperceive drawings, so that an upturned hat is seen as a plate, or a telephone is seen as a petrol can. In addition, although visual tracking of moving objects remains unimpaired, there is difficulty in transferring fixation from one point to another.

Although frontal lobe lesions can affect visual search, their most obvious effect on the person are in terms of what can be generally referred to as personality. Surgical intervention, in which the connections between the frontal lobes and the rest of the cortex are cut, has been used to cure excessively morbid thought processes. If the frontal lobes are accidentally damaged the ability to plan behaviour becomes impaired, and the individual is likely to show impulsive and unrestrained behaviour. Such clients may be able to behave independently, but they always strike one as being somewhat irresponsible and impetuous. Performance on maze problems has also been observed to be impaired in frontal lobe syndrome, and this has implications for orientation ability.

OTHER CORTICAL AREAS

When a person suffers brain damage due to stroke or to head injury it is unlikely that they will experience just one specific deficit. Rather, they will tend to experience problems in perceiving, thinking, feeling and behaving. So that multiple impairment is the rule rather than the exception. For this reason it is important that we consider other areas of the brain which are responsible for specific functions, because nature's experiments on brain damage tend to be somewhat sloppy compared to those of the neuroscientist, resulting more often than not in a combination of deficits rather than one specific one.

The left hemisphere

The brain can be thought of as consisting of two halves (hemispheres), a left and a right, joined together by a structure called the corpus callosum (literally a thick body), which can be seen in Figure 5.2, and is shaded in the exploded view in Figure 5.6. The corpus callosum transmits information between the two hemispheres, permitting different types of representation of incoming information to take place. In most right-handed people, especially males, the left side of the brain is specialized to process speech and language, both in terms of decoding the speech sounds made by others, and

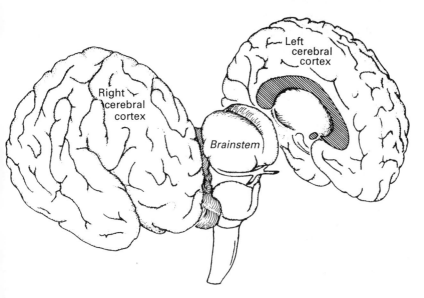

Figure 5.6 The two cerebral hemispheres.

in formulating the complex motor programmes responsible for the production of speech. When the left hemisphere is damaged due to, say, a stroke, the most likely impairment will be to some aspect of speech or language.

These impairments are collectively known as the *aphasias* (*a* – without; *phasia* – speech), or *dysphasias* (*dys* – faulty) if they are less than complete deficits, and they fall into two types. The first is caused by damage towards the front of the left hemisphere, and this is known as Broca's aphasia after the nineteenth century physician who first described it. Broca's aphasia consists of an inability to retrieve the word one is looking for. In their attempts to compensate for this type of aphasia, people often resort to circumlocutions in order to make themselves understood. Broca's aphasia is most frustrating for the sufferer as he knows what he wants to say but cannot find the words, and when he hears himself saying the wrong words he can become distressed if he is unable to correct himself.

The second type of aphasia is known as Wernicke's aphasia, after its discoverer. In contrast to the sufferer of Broca's aphasia, the sufferer of Wernicke's aphasia is unable to comprehend what other people are saying, or finds herself unable to concentrate on other people's speech because of other background sounds which interrupt the processing of speech sounds. Again, the condition is highly frustrating for the sufferer, and although there is no impairment to the intellect, to the uninitiated it appears that this is in fact the case, and sufferers are often hurtfully treated as if they were stupid, a situation in which the hard of hearing often find themselves placed by ignorant members of the public.

Because strokes do not limit themselves neatly to any specific structure of the brain, many left temporal stroke patients also have an involvement of the motor strip, producing a slurring of speech. Patients with aphasias are likely to improve dramatically just as a function of the passage of time, although speech therapy can hasten the process and result in a better quality of speech and a higher level of functioning than would be the case if there was no intervention at all.

The right hemisphere

If the left hemisphere can be characterized as the verbal one, then the right can be characterized as the spatial one, if such crude distinctions can be upheld. There is plenty of evidence to suggest that damage to the parieto-occipital areas of the right hemisphere produces deficits in orientation and spatial behaviour generally. Patients with damage to these areas have great difficulty in keeping track of where they are going, and are often found wandering about hospital wards unable to find their way back to their beds. They are unable to make use of maps and they may be unable to work out the time on clocks with hands, although digital clocks may pose no problem.

Left-sided visual neglect is another feature of right-sided parieto-occipital lesions, and sufferers are unaware of objects or people positioned to the left of the midline. Unlike cases of a right-sided visual neglect caused by damage to the left occipital cortex, people suffering from left-sided neglect cannot be trained to attend to this area of space with any guarantee of success, and the condition tends to stay with them for the remainder of their lives. A dressing apraxia (*a* – not; *praxis* – ability) often accompanies this spatial deficit and it stems from an inability to perceive the left side of the body. Such patients can often be found with one arm in the right sleeve of their jacket but with the jacket hanging from the right shoulder, or they might have put a shoe on the right foot but still have a slipper on the left.

Until comparatively recently, left-sided neglect was regarded as an intractable problem, but systematic treatment by clinical psychologists (Weinberg, Diller, Gordon *et al.*, 1977) using cueing techniques has been shown to produce a significant improvement. The authors stress the utility of this technique, not only in making the person more aware of his or her problem, but also in providing a measurable improvement in performance, although a complete cure cannot really be claimed. However, as we have seen in the previous chapter, if the client cannot be trained to attend to the neglected side, there are aids which can be of benefit.

In addition to linguistic and spatial deficits, hemispheric damage can also produce motor impairments such as weakness or paralysis of the limb on the opposite side of the hemisphere affected. This pattern of deficit is simply due to the fact that the motor nerves cross over the body at the level of the neck, but it must be considered in terms of its effects on independence training. Gait can be affected markedly, producing unsteadiness or an inability to raise the foot sufficiently. A fear of stumbling is often present and the raised tactile surfaces installed at Pelican crossings and dropped kerbs present a real danger to these people. Clumsiness, or weakness in a limb resulting in minor accidents is also a feature of hemispheric damage.

The frontal lobes

Right at the front of the brain, lying immediately behind the forehead, lie the frontal lobes, one in each hemisphere. Their role in visual perception has been noted in passing, but they play a more general role as well. One of their functions is to regulate the levels of arousal produced in the subcortical areas, and they play an important role in the voluntary direction of attention. Since control of attention is a basic psychological function in relation to learning, damage anywhere in this area has profound implications for the client.

Additionally, the frontal lobes are also involved in the conscious planning and control of sequences of action. This means that if a client is suffering from any damage to the frontal lobes he will find it difficult to carry out a complex sequence of actions, and will tend to forget what he was in the process of doing. In addition, because the frontal lobes can inhibit primitive impulses, damage in this region can disinhibit antisocial behaviour. People exhibiting the full-blown frontal lobe syndrome are characteristically carefree, and they often appear to act in an immature and impulsive way, heedless of the consequences of their behaviour.

If the damage extends to the whole of each frontal lobe, even further deficits can be observed. Not only will the client lose control over sequences of actions, but he will no longer be able to direct his actions by means of verbal prompting, either from himself or from an external source. Even more seriously, he will be unable to check to find out if the actions he has performed have produced the desired results. Such a client can never be considered to be independent, because no matter how well he copes with individual tasks, he will be unable to chain together a sequence of actions to produce the ultimate end point of the activity.

Finally, clients with intact visual systems can still show deficits in performance based on visual tasks as a consequence of frontal lobe damage. For example, if such a client is shown an illustration depicting the end point in a sequence of actions, he is likely to seize upon the first detail that captures his attention, and arrive at a premature and erroneous conclusion. If his eye movements are examined they will be found to be inadequate, whole areas of the picture being ignored, and this explains his failure to consider important details of the whole scene.

CONCLUSIONS

Although we have only barely touched upon the structure and function of the brain, it is hoped that this over-simplified account will nonetheless enable workers who have received no specific training in neuropsychology to understand better why certain individuals may exhibit particular types of otherwise puzzling behaviour. The brain is a very complicated structure, and it takes many years of study to understand it adequately. It is hoped that the simplified picture presented here suffices to give an outline of its functions without doing too much violence to the specific details involved.

In this chapter quite a lot of ground has been covered, some of which has of necessity been heavy-going. But rehabilitation workers need to know a certain amount of neuropsychology in order to make sense of some of their clients' problems, and to be able to talk to other professionals such as psychologists or occupational therapists about how they can each in their own way help the client. Also, they need to be able to hazard an intelligent guess as to what might be going on when other professionals are unavailable, and to get on with the job of assessing the client's residual functioning and implementing a realistic rehabilitation programme without outside help. Those of you who regularly encounter clients with brain damage should consult Goldstein and Ruthven (1983) for a fuller account of how to rehabilitate them.

The following chapter will look at some real-life cases of clients who have suffered from brain damage in addition to a visual impairment. In this way, it is hoped that the reader will see the relevance of the material presented in this chapter. It is also hoped that the contents of this chapter have stimulated readers' interest in a topic of limitless fascination, and that some of the references will be followed up, providing more detailed information for those readers whose appetites may have been whetted.

6

Special client groups and their problems

A number of visually impaired clients, particularly elderly ones, are likely to possess one or more additional impairments, making the task of rehabilitation even more difficult for you both. Common difficulties are a hearing impairment, or the presence of a physical disability which may restrict movement and make it difficult to master standard techniques. As these additional impairments present their own specific challenges, not necessarily of a psychological nature, this chapter will not attempt to deal with them in any detail. Those of you requiring such information are recommended to consult Erin (1989) on how to deal with multiple disabilities.

In spite of the fact that a dual sensory impairment is common among elderly people, no single textbook addresses this neglected area. Those of you who require information on the rehabilitation of the deaf/blind client are recommended to read Schein (1986) and a list of useful papers by practitioners containing practical guidelines can be obtained in the United Kingdom from the reference librarian of the RNIB. However, there are clients who fall into special categories who present rehabilitation workers with considerable problems which are strictly psychological, and this chapter will deal with those as they are fairly common and require some detailed knowledge unavailable to most workers.

THE BRAIN-DAMAGED CLIENT

Like most of life's woes, brain damage tends to visit a person not singly, but in battalions. This often makes the task of assessment difficult if not daunting. However, by being aware of the various parts of the brain and their function it is possible, although not always easy, to identify the client's difficulties and help him understand and come to terms with his problem. In the absence of clinical case notes, the best that you can do is to establish what the client can do by placing him in a wide variety of situations and observing his performance. Then simply try to teach him the skills he needs. If you get stuck, consult a textbook on neuropsychological rehabilitation (e.g. Goldstein and Ruthven, 1983; Meier, Benton and Diller, 1987; Wood and Fussey, 1990). If you still cannot make sense of things, then seek a psychological opinion or the assistance of an occupational therapist who will be well-acquainted with the problems associated with brain damage.

Many clients have a visual impairment or have been blinded as a result of having been involved in a road traffic accident which has physically damaged a part of the brain. Others may have suffered a stroke or a cardiac arrest which could have temporarily starved parts of the brain of oxygen. More rarely, a client could have had a brain tumour which has affected the visual system, or they might have overdosed on some drug or other, or have received some medication to which they have responded adversely. In these latter cases the damage may be quite diffuse, producing generalized brain damage and causing varying degrees of learning difficulty. The previous chapter described how different parts of the brain were responsible for different functions, and what the results of brain damage can be; this chapter examines a number of real-life examples of clients whose brains have been affected in different ways. These cases will illustrate the importance of an elementary knowledge of brain function and will give a general idea of how to proceed during the initial stages of assessment.

Case 1

I was once asked to help staff at a rehabilitation centre who were baffled by a client whom we shall call Alex: a man in his early forties who had suffered a stroke. Formal visual testing proved impossible because he was unable to see the

Snellen chart on the wall, or even the face of the tester. During repeated attempts to read the top line in the chart, he said that he thought he had seen the word 'Greensmith'. I asked him if that was the name of a person or a place, but he was unable to recognize the meaning of the name, or to say where he had seen it. Looking around the room for clues, I noticed a piece of equipment bearing the name 'Smith' in small, green letters. It is likely that this was the stimulus for the response that he produced, but it illustrated that he could see colour and had an acuity approaching normal in some portion of his visual field, although he did not have the experience of seeing.

Outdoors, he could walk along the road with relative ease without a cane and appeared to be aware of quite a number of features of the environment. He did not trip at kerbs and seemed able to avoid obstacles and pick out landmarks. So what could he see, and how could one find out? On passing a cottage in the other side of the road, I asked him if he could read the name on the door. He partly guessed 'Hillside', when in fact it was 'Woodside', but this information was quite consistent with that obtained accidentally in the vision testing room, in that he could see over a very limited area and that his acuity in this area was approaching normal.

In the course of an hour's mobility lesson I observed his behaviour, asking him to report on anything he saw or thought he saw, because it was not clear to him whether he was really seeing or simply imagining. 'There's a bird,' he announced as we walked past a large house. 'Can you tell me more about it?' I asked. 'It's a bird near the fire,' he replied. 'I don't understand,' I said. 'What do you mean by *near the fire*?' 'Where the smoke goes,' he answered. 'Oh, I see,' I replied. 'You mean a chimney?' 'Yes, thank you very much,' he said. I looked up, and noticed a seagull perched on one of the chimneys of the house. 'Can you tell me what kind of bird it is?' I asked. 'A pigeon that lives by the sea,' he replied. 'Good,' I said. 'You can see a seagull sitting 30 feet away. That proves beyond doubt that your residual sight is going to be much better than any mobility aid yet invented, even if you don't yet believe that you are seeing'.

Alex had occipital cortical damage combined with damage to the left hemisphere. The two conspired to make him severely handicapped. He was virtually totally blind at a conscious level, so that although some parts of his visual system were intact, little or none of the information was experienced visually. However, it did reach his consciousness although he could not say how it did. There must have been little holes in his blindness through which tiny fragments of the world came, but his aphasia produced by the left hemisphere damage made it difficult to take at face value what he reported. This meant that almost every statement had to be checked out by restating to him what he had said, often using different words in order to get his agreement about precisely what he had meant to express.

Here is a good example of a client who was multiply handicapped and who presented the assessor with a host of problems. In order to find out what is going on, one normally has to rely on what your client tells you. But a client who has a speech output problem is unable to give accurate reports because he cannot find the right words. He needs to be helped out in this respect. In addition, because he did not have the experience of seeing, there were no grounds for him having any confidence in what he reported. Again, someone lacking in confidence needs to have your belief in the validity of what they are saying if you have good reason to believe that they have grounds for making their statements.

Finally, because parts of his visual system were processing the information correctly without his awareness, Alex was unable to tell the difference between imagining that he had seen something and actually having seen something. This may be a subtle point to grasp, but think of how a sighted person could tell if they were imagining or seeing something. If they were to close their eyes and the image remained, then they would conclude that they were imagining something. If they closed their eyes and it disappeared, then they would conclude that they were seeing something. But Alex did not have that crucial test available: closing his eyes made no difference whatsoever to his conscious experience, so that he could validly conclude that he was imagining the things which were there and which he was aware of.

Little wonder that he was totally confused to the extent of being in fear of his sanity. One of the most valuable contributions which the psychologist had to make was to reassure this client that he was perfectly sane and that his strange combination of problems, rare as they were, could be understood, and also to tell the rehabilitation team that their suspicions about his sight were justified. The next task was to plan his rehabilitation programme in the light of these and other assessment findings. Although two years on from his rehabilitation Alex is not in employment, and he has been advised that medical retirement is his best option. After receiving counselling, he has accepted this, and the quality of his life has thereby been vastly improved by the efforts of the various members of the rehabilitation team.

Strokes and brain tumours can produce a bewildering combination of deficits which tend to obscure one another. Your task is that of trying to disentangle the various impairments from one another, and this can be a considerable challenge. If you should find yourself unable to make sense of your client's performance, then do seek advice from a clinical neuropsychologist. These people can often be found attached to stroke or head injury units, and the staff there have a detailed knowledge of brain damage coupled with a wide variety of psychological tests which can help pinpoint particular areas of difficulty. In the United Kingdom, the Royal National Institute for the Blind has a head-injury support network comprising a number of experts who will be prepared to discuss difficult cases over the telephone and to put you in touch with the appropriate person in your area.

Case 2

When I was training as a mobility instructor I had the good fortune to be given a number of clients who had additional problems, and I learned a lot from them. One such client had suffered extensive brain damage as a result of having had recurrent tumours removed. As these had involved the optic nerve, John, as we shall call him, was totally blind. The areas which had been involved were deep in the midbrain, and as a result the structures responsible for attention and memory had been severely affected, as had parts of his frontal lobes.

As a consequence of this extensive damage, John's eating was out of control, and he was very overweight. His movements were extremely slow, and he gave the appearance of being 'elsewhere' in his mind. If he was not engaged in conversation, he would sit immobile, except for a few repetitive finger movements which seemed to have no purpose. On introducing myself, he gave a startle response, and asked who I was. I informed him that we would be doing mobility together, and that I would see him the next day.

On the following day, when I introduced myself to him again, he showed no recognition of my name, nor recollection of our conversation the day before. This was to become a familiar pattern: I would introduce myself to him and he would greet me as if we had only just met. Although he soon responded in a familiar way to the sound of my voice, in 12 weeks he never did manage to remember my name. This indicated to me that although John had no recall, he did have recognition, and that he might be expected to learn something, although at that stage it was not clear what.

I took him for a walk sighted guide on each successive day, in order to get to know him and to assess what residual functioning he had. He had already acquired a reputation among the staff for being lazy, unco-operative and aggressive, and I felt that he was not receiving the credit for anything he might be trying to do and that his difficulties, which were clearly beyond his control, were being attributed to wilfulness. I realized that I would have to act as advocate for him, and that in order to do justice to this role, a comprehensive psychological assessment was necessary. Rather than spend hours sitting with him carrying out formal psychological tests, I chose to go about the assessment concurrently with trying to teach him mobility.

When I began to teach John a route from his room to the toilet, it became apparent to me that he would drift off into a 'fugue' from which it would be difficult for me to extract him. A fugue is a state of mental wandering, and during these states John was inaccessible. I eventually hit upon the strategy of simply allowing the fugue to overtake him, but of jolting him out of it after a minute or so by snapping my fingers loudly in his ear. Talking to him produced no response, but the mild audible shock seemed to switch his attention back on again. He would then apologize for having drifted off and would ask me to remind him of what I had been saying. This technique, which we worked out between us, enabled me to concentrate my teaching within moments when I had his attention.

During one of our lessons with the guide cane, I inadvertently placed unrealistic demands upon him, and he lost his temper and lashed out in my direction. As he was over six feet tall and weighed over 250 pounds, I became quite nimble on my feet, and adept at reading the signs which preceded such uncontrollable outbursts. Sometimes, instead of lashing out, he would burst into tears out of sheer frustration, and I learned to accept these emotional outbursts as part and parcel of his regular behaviour. I now began to understand why some of the staff had labelled him so negatively, and made a point of taking openly about his problems in the staffroom in the hope that this would change the views of those who believed that he was simply being awkward.

After 12 weeks, John was able to walk safely along the pavement to some nearby shops, although he could never work out how to get back again. Since he was not expected to live for very much longer, the whole business of mobility training might have seemed to some a waste of time. But he did learn a number of the basic skills, and he enjoyed his walks to the shops and the opportunity that those afforded him for conversation. In spite of the massive brain damage he had received, there were moments when he could be remarkably lucid and insightful. Without the slightest hint of self-pity, he informed me one day that he would have liked to have known me in the days when he was all right. That convinced me that our time together had not been wasted, and that rehabilitation had been able to improve the quality of the remaining months of his life, as well as teaching me just how intact the person can remain in the face of such deficits.

Case 3

Jane was an outgoing lady in her mid-30s. She had suffered a personal tragedy, and she had tried to put an end to her suffering by shooting herself through the head, the latter of which she had managed successfully to do. Had a neighbour not been in her garden at the time, heard the shot and telephoned for an ambulance, she would not have survived. As luck would have it, the bullet had entered one temple and exited from the other, and she was left externally with only two tiny scars which could not be seen beneath her hair.

However, her external appearance belied the damage which had been done inside her head. She was now totally blind, as the bullet had severed the optic nerve, and in spite of the tragic circumstances surrounding her loss of sight, she showed no signs of depression or self-recrimination. In fact, it would be true to say that she often appeared to be quite euphoric. I later discovered that the bullet had also partially severed the frontal lobes of her brain, so that this impression fitted in well with what we learned in Chapter 5 about the role of this area of the brain.

Jane was very intelligent and eager to regain her independence. On the face of it, she appeared to be an ideal candidate for the long cane, and this proved to be the case. She was always ready for the lesson before I appeared, and she showed a high level of enthusiasm and a ready facility to learn. She would often practise outside lesson times and she quickly became proficient. Within only a few weeks she was travelling independently to the nearby shops, and on returning home on the occasional weekend, would show off her newly-acquired mobility skills to her newly-acquired boyfriend. She also became highly literate in Braille and equally proficient at other independent living skills.

In spite of her high levels of intelligence and motivation, teaching did occasionally prove problematic. Given what we know about the role of the frontal lobes in relation to the inhibition of impulses and the planning of sequences of actions, it came as no surprise to me when Jane would suddenly take off in the middle of a set of instructions that I was giving her, and walk briskly off into the middle distance, only to stop at the first down-kerb unsure of what she should do next. With perseverance on both sides, however, this problem became much more manageable, although she tended to remain an impulsive person in other areas of her life.

THE CLIENT WITH LEARNING DIFFICULTIES

An impairment in intellectual functioning can produce a learning disability whose severity is proportional to the impairment. Learning difficulties used to be known as 'mental subnormality', but negative labels serve only to decrease expectations, and the idea of a person having difficulty in acquiring new skills is better served by a label which indicates the need for special considerations during teaching, such as a slower pace and the opportunity for repeated practice with praise for success, than by one which lowers goals.

Learning difficulties can range from mild, where the client simply appears to require more time, practice and explanation during learning, to profound where he appears unable to grasp a simple idea or is unable to put together a sequence of instructions. Some causes of learning difficulty may give the client a strange appearance, or may result in odd mannerisms. Conditions such as autism, where the person experiences considerable stress in the presence of other people or of changing environments, make it difficult for the rehabilitation worker to proceed in her usual manner. Autistic clients may appear socially awkward or unable to relate to the task in hand, yet they can have islands of very high ability, often being musically or artistically talented, and their abilities should not be underestimated on the superficial basis of appearance.

Possessing a low measured intelligence has a direct bearing on learning ability, and this is true almost by definition. But one should not be too dismissive of the potential for rehabilitation for individuals with a low IQ. Those who score above 35 (the norm is 100) are probably below the ability to improve their functioning, but even those with an IQ in the 50s are likely to show a measureable improvement with systematic training where simple goals are set. By carrying out a task analysis, complex sequences of behaviour can be broken down into elementary units which are then taught individually. Once these have been mastered, the units can then be combined to form a chain of responses. In this way, sequences of actions which could not be grasped as a whole can be learned. Those of you who would like to know more about behavioural methods for training should consult McBrien and Foxen (1981), whereas more cognitive methods can be found in Solberg and Mateer (1989).

Adults with learning difficulties may not be able to understand the point of their rehabilitation, and they may not be able to take responsibility for their own learning. Given this, it would be unrealistic to expect them to set their own long-term goals, although their contribution to the setting of short-term goals should be encouraged from the outset. Only if they show an inability to do this should goals be set on their behalf. Expect short spans of attention and set attainable goals within that span. Try to find out the limits of attentional span and also try to increase these by means of reminding the client how far along the task he is, and give encouragement and lots of praise when he succeeds with any sub-goal within the overall plan. A fuller explanation of goal-setting is presented in Chapter 8.

Some clients with learning difficulties appear immature and emotionally childish. They may laugh at inappropriate moments, or they may be unable to engage in self-control, having tantrums or tears. They may go to pieces under pressure or show challenging behaviour. Only after considerable experience with such a client will you find yourself in a position to judge how best to relate to them. Expect to have to do most of the work in this respect, and remain flexible, as some clients may vary considerably from day to day, depending on their experiences in the interim (Dickens and Stallard, 1987). Keep objective records of goals achieved in order to remind yourself that progress, albeit gradual, is taking place. Those of you who regularly deal with clients with learning difficulties should consult Booth (1990) and Booth, Simons and Roth (1990), and you should also try to cultivate a sympathetic psychologist who can help you plan your teaching better.

THE HYSTERICALLY BLIND CLIENT

Almost all of of you will at some time in your working lives come across a client whose diagnosis is functional or hysterical blindness. As you go about the business of assessing each client, you may form the impression that they are able to behave in ways which might suggest cortical blindness, in that they may be able to avoid obstacles and to detect down-kerbs, yet appear unable to identify objects or recognize people. You may doubt that the label 'hysterical blindness' is the correct one, and that the person is really unable to see consciously.

Opthalmological examination is able to differentiate between cortical and hysterical blindness because it is impossible to inhibit reflex behaviour. The 'menace response' (blinking at the approach of a threatening visual stimulus) is absent in cortical blindness but present in hysterical blindness. Similarly, the optokinetic response (the eyes automatically follow a rotating, striped drum jerkily) is absent in the former but present in the latter. However, if you do not have access to opthalmological information, you can carry out a few simple tests yourself, because there are clues which, taken together, point to hysterical rather than cortical blindness.

The first is the likelihood that the hysterically blind client will prefer to wear very dark glasses, possibly with side-shades attached to them. The purpose of wearing these is two-fold. In the first place, it gives out a social signal to sighted people that the wearer is blind. Secondly, it conceals the person's eyes from the gaze of others, and enables them to look about at relevant aspects of the environment without this being detected. You should therefore ask the client to take their glasses off. If they comply, watch their eye movements to see if they avoid your gaze. If they do, then the chances are that they can see. If they refuse, suspect the worst, but such simple little give-aways should be noted.

In addition, it is important to give yourself as many opportunities as possible to observe the client's behaviour in a variety of situations, because hysterically blind people behave neither like sighted, partially sighted nor totally blind people. In order to establish the presence of hysterical blindness, one must try to catch the client out without giving the message that one does not trust them or that one is in any way passing judgement on them. This is difficult to sustain on perhaps more than one or two occasions without arousing their suspicions and preventing a trusting relationship from developing, but it is possible if one is subtle.

The simplest approach is to take the client for a long walk along a quiet road without the assistance of a sighted guide, explaining that there is no danger involved and that you will be right beside them all the time. Hysterically blind people tend to be highly suggestible and are likely to go along with such a proposal. As you approach a down-kerb, keep walking yourself and step into the road. Watch for the client slowing down and then feeling for the kerb with their foot, because if they do this, it indicates that they have perceived the kerb visually, but want you to think that they have to feel for it. On questioning, the client will make up some vague or implausible story about why they stopped, such as sensing danger.

Another good test is to let the client think that you are not keeping proper watch over their safety. This can be achieved by appearing somewhat nonchalant, or looking at something of passing interest. A usual response is for them to stage a minor accident for your benefit, such as veering off course and colliding with a lamp-post, or tripping down a flight of steps. In the latter situation, be sure you can catch them in case they stage a major fall, because at that point they are really testing your concern for them, and they may be prepared to risk physical injury in order to prove to themselves that you do not really believe that they are blind.

Hysterically blind clients often alienate themselves from the rehabilitator. They tend to come over as rather pathetic malingerers, yet they have a real psychological need for approval and a terrible fear of being found out. The alienation springs from their need to deceive, and it is hard to build up trust between these two people when one of them is not being honest. And yet they are being as honest as possible, given the pain of their own perceived inadequacy. The psychological mechanisms which cause them to deny their sight are protecting a part of them which is very hurt indeed, and the last thing they require is further judgment being passed on them. But the cost of maintaining the illusion of blindness must be very great and such clients must be under immense stress as a result of trying to maintain the appearance of being blind.

The most you may be able to do for such clients is to give them a sense of self-worth. Use all of the techniques described in Chapter 8, praising their achievements and encouraging any insights which they may have. If they volunteer information about their private lives, listen attentively and try to deal with it yourself, particularly if you have received training in counselling. But if you find yourself getting out of your depth, hand over the work to a trained professional such as a full-time counsellor, therapist, clinical psychologist or psychiatrist, depending upon whom might be available.

Psychologists have had some success in getting hysterically blind people to acknowledge that they are able to behave visually by progressively lightening the lenses in their spectacles, so that eventually they end up with clear glass. At this point it may become possible to test the client's acuity and field, and to prescribe an appropriate correction. Many hysterically blind people do have a genuine visual defect of a fairly minor nature which they seize upon as a psychological crutch. Once this has been removed, and they can see that they are able to perform visually in a safe and accepting environment, it may be possible to rehabilitate them sufficiently for them to be able to continue visually after rehabilitation.

It must be said, however, that the elaborate illusion of blindness, particularly if it has been allowed to go on for some years, is difficult to throw off. One does hear of cases where a hysterically blind person has regained their sight after suffering an accident as minor as tripping over their guide dog. At such a point the individual must recognize that the cost of maintaining the illusion outweighs the benefits, and desperately seeks a face-saving *volte-face*. Newspapers love stories like this, as they come under the heading of 'sentimental', and help pad out a thin copy. But as noted in Chapter 1, such publicity only holds out false hopes to those who are genuinely and permanently without sight.

I remember being confused once on being introduced to a gentleman who claimed that he had met me several years before at a party. Unable to recall him for some time precisely, I suddenly realized that this was due to the fact that he had then been introduced to me as a totally blind person, but that he was now normally sighted! He informed me that while he had been 'blind' he had amazed his friends by piloting his narrow boat through canal locks which he managed to operate himself. How he knew whether to jump up or down from the boat to the lock gate had been a mystery to all who knew him. I spared him as well as myself the embarrassment of further conversation. Some stones are best left unturned, even by psychologists.

THE DISFIGURED CLIENT

Diseases and disorders of the eye can often produce external manifestations which render the sufferer conspicuous in advance of any interaction having taken place or any activity having been performed which may indicate that the person needs to be treated with special consideration. The client whose eyes continually water and look red is often mistakenly regarded as someone who is upset and crying as a result. In ignorance of the true cause of the flow of tears, well-meaning people may offer sympathy and amateur counselling to a person who is simply troubled by continual irritation of the eyes. Not that they do not deserve sympathy; it is just the wrong kind of sympathy that they receive.

A client who has suffered a loss of sight through trauma may bear evidence of this in the form of scarring or quite obvious disfigurement. People who pass through the windscreen of an automobile at high speed are likely to have lost some or all of their sight: if they have not then they can count themselves lucky. But they may have had to undergo considerable facial reconstructive surgery to restore ears, eyelids, nose, lips and so on. Such people may look strange or even repellant to those unused to seeing anything other than a 'normal' face. The World Health Organisation classifies disfigurement as a separate category of impairment, so that the visually impaired client who possesses a disfigurement should be considered as suffering from a dual impairment.

A client who has lost his sight through trauma of this nature may not understand that his appearance has altered radically as a result of his accident. He will, however, slowly begin to discover that social interactions are more difficult than he remembered them to be, and he may initially attribute this to his loss of sight, hoping that he will develop skills based on reading intonations in voices and noting pauses in conversations which will make interactions flow more smoothly. Eventually, he will have to face the fact that the problem may lie elsewhere, and at this point he may begin to ask how he actually looks. The courage required to ask such a question indicates that he is ready to hear the worst, and this is a positive sign, but the information needs to be accompanied by a sensitive response to his feelings.

In the case of a sighted person, facial disfigurement results in a number of emotions being experienced (Partridge, 1990). These are not unlike the emotions being experienced as a result of loss of sight, such as anger, misery and repulsion. But there is a crucial difference: the blind client is unlikely to be able to experience his appearance directly, and he must make guesses about it on the basis of questioning a sighted person. In order to spare his feelings, the sighted person might try to minimize the degree of disfigurement, but this is not going to help in the long run as other sighted people are still going to react in the same way. So that if you are going to be honest, you must possess the counselling skills necessary to help your client come to terms with the situation. You may also have to examine your own reactions and make adjustments to your own feelings if you are to be of maximum help.

Although all facial reconstructive units have counsellors and psychologists on their staff who are likely to have seen your client before you do, not all of them have the understanding of visual impairment which you have. With your knowledge of the difficulties which blind people can normally expect to experience in this area, you will be able to assess how much of your client's difficulties may be due to the disfigurement. If necessary, it may be appropriate to have your client referred back to the hospital with a view to providing a better prosthesis or carrying out further work in order to make his appearance more socially acceptable. In the United Kingdom, a charitable organization called 'Changing Faces' (see Appendix) specializes in giving disfigured people social skills training and counselling where no further physical improvement is possible.

THE AIDS CLIENT

Acquired Immune Deficiency Syndrome (AIDS) develops over a long period of time, and the incubation period may be as long as 11 years between initial infection and the onset of the syndrome. The syndrome represents the final stage of infection with human immunodeficiency virus (HIV). One of the many common AIDS-related visual disorders is cytomegalovirus (CMV) retinitis, which is a late-stage opportunist infection (Daugherty, 1988; Keister, 1990). This means that anybody who is developing CMV retinitis is now likely to have had the full-blown AIDS syndrome for three or four years, and that they may have been infected with HIV for anything up to 15 years.

As recently as a year ago the prognosis would have been pretty poor by the time CMV had been diagnosed, and death would have followed within months. Now, with the improved treatment of AIDS-related conditions, life expectancy is increasing as new combinations of drugs are found. This means that if you are to have any involvement with such a client you have to get in as soon as possible after CMV is diagnosed in order to have the maximum impact. But you must be prepared to have your feelings hurt because your client is going to die. If you are going to be of any real help you will have to give a lot of yourself and as a result you will have formed a special relationship whose end will be emotionally painful.

Precisely what you can do will depend upon the client's physical condition. This can vary enormously between clients, some of them being fit enough to walk short distances, others being too weak to undertake more than a few steps across the room. What independent living skills you do teach should be determined by negotiation with the client, and the goal-setting techniques described in Chapter 8 should be employed. Knowing that one is likely to die before a cure for the illness is found is a deeply depressing prospect for a person who, like the rest of us, may have believed that he would be allotted his three-score years and ten, and to lose one's sight before finally losing one's life must feel like an additional and unnecessary cruelty.

If you have had counselling training this may enable you to provide the client with the acceptance and caring which they may so desperately need, although existing 'buddy' systems may render such intervention unecessary. Attitudes towards AIDS-infected people tend to be shaped by stereotypes prevalent in society and homophobic attitudes may make gay men feel isolated and rejected. Others may be drug-users, or they could have been infected through a blood transfusion rather than by any identifiable individual. But since most CMV sufferers are likely to be gay men and drug users, as these were the groups first infected with HIV, you may need to examine your own attitudes towards these factors before deciding on whether you can offer unconditional and truly professional support.

Dying people may be grieving not only for themselves, but for close friends and relatives whom they know they will leave behind, so that grief therapy can be appropriate here. Cognitive therapy may be indicated if the person appears unable to accept the inevitable, and a clinical psychologist experienced with such groups should be sought from the area health authority if the person is not already receiving expert counselling. Along with grief may be outbursts of aggressive feelings towards a person or persons believed to be responsible for the infection. Alternating rage and depression may overwhelm the individual, depleting their energies further, and you need to develop an ability to deal with these strong feelings without cutting yourself off emotionally from the person. None of this is easy, and you may well require emotional support yourself. In the United Kingdom, the Terence Higgins Trust (see Appendix) provides information of a non-medical nature on HIV/AIDS.

In this chapter, the needs of clients who are suffering from more than just a visual impairment have been examined. In many cases, 'visually impaired' is simply a misleading label, as the client's needs may be related only loosely to their visual status. It is unfortunate that people acquire labels, but unless thay are initially labelled in some way, the helping professions cannot legitimately become involved. Labels may indeed flag up the need for help, but they may also invite a response to the label which may not be in the client's best interest. Paradoxically, labelling often tends to handicap the person even more, particularly once their immediate needs have been met. After that, labels serve no further use, and people should then be treated on their own merits in ways which enable them to take control of their own lives, or to come to terms with what cannot be controlled.

7

Congenital blindness

Losing one's sight after having lived for years as a sighted person presents the individual with an extraordinary variety of difficulties, which have now been examined in some detail. However, being born without sight presents the person with a completely different set of problems, many of which have gone unappreciated. The main problem for us as sighted people is that of understanding what it must be like to live in a sighted world without ever having been able to share a set of sensory experiences with the majority of those who inhabit it. Thus one of the primary difficulties we have when dealing with the independence needs of a congenitally blind person is that of not being able to enter into their world of experience. This effectively places a communication barrier between us and our client.

This difficulty should not be underestimated, and it can be the source of many confusions and misconceptions. Nor will an extended wearing of the blindfold in any way enable one to enter into the mind of a congenitally blind person. It may enable one to understand the problems of monitoring and keeping track of movements which a totally blind traveller experiences, but it will not provide any insights into how someone who has never seen the world deals with these problems. Only carefully conducted research can reveal the ways in which such people represent the world around them, and even then, the research often raises more questions than it answers. But at least it should teach us what questions can or cannot be answered, and what the answers might mean in terms of practical help.

A number of writers have examined cases of total congenital blindness in an attempt to answer what are properly philosophical as opposed to psychological questions, such as whether or not a person without sight can ever conceive of space. Such questions go back a number of centuries, and philosophers of various persuasion have considered instances of congenital blindness to provide support or otherwise for the assertion that spatial concepts can develop only as a result of experience. Unfortunately, the subjective reports of the people interviewed are unable to provide any definitive answer, and with hindsight, it is easy to see how ill-conceived many of these questions have been. Those of you of a philosophical disposition might find von Senden's *Space and Sight* (1960) and Morgan's *Molyneux's Question* (1977) enjoyable bedtime reading.

Interesting as such philosophical conjectures have been, many of them do not really make much sense even at a common sense level. For example, Bower (1977) claimed that a congenitally blind child has the greatest difficulty in mastering even the simplest spatial concept. Without considering what a concept is, what it is to possess a concept, or further to consider what a spatial concept might be, statements of this nature are unhelpful at a theoretical level and can be damaging at a practical one.

If we consider a congenitally blind traveller finding the bus stop, undertaking a journey and finding his way back again (quite a commonplace occurrence), it is simply perverse to claim that he has no concept of space. A more interesting question might be how his conceptualization might differ from that of a sighted person, or from that of a person who was once sighted but who is now no longer. The net effect of making negative statements about congenitally blind people is that when we do find that they have problems we are tempted to write them off as being insoluble rather than to use our imaginations to try to find solutions.

There is a parallel to be drawn here with respect to the way in which society used to treat Down syndrome people as being congenitally incapable of learning to speak, and of being ineducable. So that one often hears rehabilitaion staff and teachers of blind children declare that the reason for a child having spatial difficulties is because he is a 'typical congenital'.

This sort of labelling simply writes off any possibility of helping the child and at the same time absolves the teacher from any responsibility for his inability to understand why the child appears unable to grasp something which his late-blinded counterpart can comprehend without difficulty. Accepting that congenital blindness may certainly place impediments in the way of spatial understanding need not force us to accept that spatial incompetence is inevitable and irremediable.

Total, congenital blindness is rare, and two causes of this condition which have been singled out for special consideration are retinoblastoma and retinopathy of prematurity. Whether individuals suffering from either one of these conditions exhibit any additional cognitive idiosyncrasies remains speculation, in spite of several attempts to show that they do. Let us consider each of these two conditions briefly.

RETINOBLASTOMA

Retinoblastoma is an inherited condition in which the cells of the retina develop chaotically, producing tumours which can rapidly infiltrate the optic nerve and invade the brain, causing death unless the eyes are enucleated as soon as the condition is diagnosed. Alert and sensitive care-givers are often the first people to suspect that there may be something wrong with their infant, and stories abound of mothers trying to convince the medical profession that they are right to be unhappy about their infant's visual behaviour.

Researchers have found that children who have retinoblastoma are significantly more intelligent than those blind from birth through some other cause (Warren, 1984). Can we therefore assume that this represents a case of a genuine increase in IQ as a direct result of the medical condition? Interesting as the conjecture is, there are simpler and more plausible common sense interpretations available to us. One could equally argue that the fact that these infants were diagnosed early and their lives were saved was due to the intelligence, educational level and social status of the parents, all of which would be likely to contribute to the intelligence of their offspring.

It is highly probable that an intelligent and well-informed care-giver would be more likely to notice some small deficiency in an infant than one who is less well-informed, and also to be able to hazard a guess at its seriousness. Middle class parents are much more likely to assert themselves when faced with disbelief from the medical profession than are those who are used to being patronized by professionals. Again, a caregiver who is constantly harrassed by the domestic scene is less likely to notice small details which could be early signs of trouble than one who has the luxury of being able to spend considerable amounts of time interacting with the infant. The IQ issue is therefore once again seen to be a hornet's nest of speculation and emotion, and as such, is best left on one side.

RETINOPATHY OF PREMATURITY

A cause of early blindness which used to be known as retrolental fibroplasia is now called retinopathy of prematurity (ROP). Its cause is the administering of excessive amounts of oxygen to the pre-term infant, producing spasm of the retinal blood vessels. This can be followed by a proliferation of blood vessels into the vitreous, resulting in total retinal detachment and hence total blindness.

One recurrent theme which one finds in the field, rather than in the literature, is that individuals suffering from congenital blindness caused by retinopathy of prematurity have additional spatial difficulties. Educationalists and O & M instructors have a definite impression that the majority of their clients who exhibit a lack of spatial understanding are those who have ROP. I have personally had two ROP clients, and indeed, they have shown strange patterns of behaviour which suggest that they may have specific gaps in their knowledge of the spatial layout of the environment, and of the spatial consequences of their own movements. But whether or not this is due to ROP itself or stems from the fact that they have never seen the environment is worth investigating.

In a small-scale study involving 11-year-old children (Dodds, Howarth and Clark-Carter, 1982), it was found that congentially blind children were significantly poorer at pointing to route locations and drawing raised maps than were their adventitiously blinded counterparts. But in a larger study of congenitally blind children which looked at the pointing behaviour of 40 children, half of whom were ROP, the other half of whom were non-ROP, no significant differences were observed (Dodds *et al.*, 1991b). So that the hypothesis that ROP carries with it an additional spatial deficit received no firm support, although the belief that total congenital blindness produces deficits in spatial understanding did.

One interpretation of the above findings is that ROP does not in itself result in an additional cognitive deficit, but that total, congenital blindness can cause parents to over protect their children and limit their exploration of the environment. Combined with this prematurity, this may be at the root of the spatial deficits observed in ROP individuals. Such an interpretation was supported by a surprisingly significant correlation between children's scores on a section of an IQ test which tested their knowledge of the world and their ability to keep track of where they were on a route. Whereas static and dynamic memory performance were unrelated to pointing behaviour, the knowledge of how real-world objects were similar to one another was highly correlated with pointing accuracy.

THE CASE OF GRAHAM O

Sometimes one can learn about more congenitally blind people by working systematically with one of them over a period of time than by carrying out brief research on large numbers of them. Although any interesting findings which may emerge cannot be generalized immediately, they can form the basis of research hypotheses which can subsequently be tested. One such totally congenitally blind client whom I had the privilege of teaching was a 33-year-old man of above average intelligence (IQ = 133). The cause of his blindness was ROP. He had a relentlessly enquiring mind, and was fascinated when I showed him how to draw using the Sewell Raised Line Kit. He recognized one of my drawings of a bicycle immediately, and I showed him how to trace round objects for himself and make his own drawings. The activity fascinated him, and he produced all manner of objects to trace, eager to show off his newly acquired skill and clearly enjoying the results.

Unfortunately, frustration soon marred his enjoyment. After he had drawn round his watch with great care, he tried to trace round the hands in order to indicate the time on the drawing. But the pen would not go through the watch onto the Melinex, and I had to draw the hands for him. He saw this as cheating, and it was a big disappointment to him that he could not produce an accurate drawing unassisted. He spent much time pondering on the problem, and I spent an equally long time trying to explain why tracing can only produce outline drawings. My explanations did not seem to produce the answer he was looking for, and he began to lose interest in drawing from that moment.

It was when we were learning the layout of two intersecting routes that the real insights began. As I was about to begin research for a doctoral thesis at the time, I freely used our mobility lessons to try out a few hunches of my own. One was that without previous sight of the environment and all the perspective transformations that vision gives, it would be difficult, if not impossible, to combine spatial information derived from two separate sources at different times. Indeed, it seemed to me that a map of the environment represented a special case of a perspective transformation, namely a bird's eye view, and that without the ability to imagine what a bird's eye view was, it would be impossible to understand a basic mapping convention.

I decided to test out these hunches with Graham, because he was so keen to try anything new and took all the tests as personal challenges. It was also legitimate orientation training, and we each enjoyed the work. Figure 7.1 illustrates the two routes used in what turned out to be a small pilot study for the small-scale experimental study described earlier. As can be seen, routes one and two are mirror-images of one

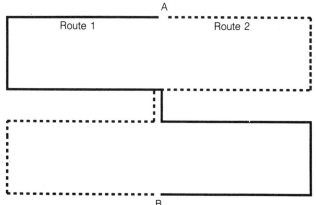

Figure 7.1 Routes used in pilot study.

another, and they represent alternative ways of travelling from A to B. I taught Graham each route separately and confirmed that he could travel them without error. Being very bright, he did this after only two trials.

Once we had walked each route three times, I showed him some details of the crossing point common to each route. On the first inner shoreline was a garden gate with a hedge beside it, and on the first outer shoreline was a wooden pole smelling strongly, as it did in the hot sun, of creosote. Beside the pole was a dustbin. On the second inner shoreline was another garden gate with a crudely built stone wall on either side. Graham felt all of these features and was happy that he could recognize them again should he encounter them.

On the next pass over route one I got him to confirm that he was at the now familiar crossing point. On the next pass over route two, at the same crossing point I asked him to

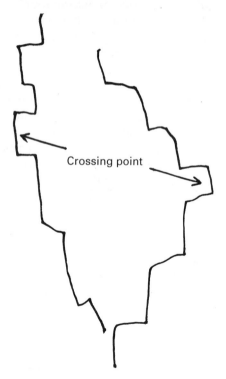

Figure 7.2 Graham's drawing of the routes.

explore the features of the first inner and outer shorelines. He expressed surprise at the coincidence of them being so like the features of the first crossing point, but did not say that they were the same point on the route. I then gave him the Sewell Raised Line Kit, with which he was now quite familiar, and asked him to draw each route on the same sheet, as they related to one another. He did this with great confidence and proudly showed me the drawing illustrated in Figure 7.2.

To the sighted eye, the routes do not appear to intersect at the common crossing point, although they are almost mirror-images of one another. I took Graham's finger over the routes, asking him to talk me through them. Although he correctly named the left and right turns (apart from the odd mistake), it was clear from his drawing that he did not appreciate that turning caused him to alter the direction of his travel. So that although the routes began and ended together, they never met in the middle. That this is not just reflecting an idiosyncratic drawing convention was exemplified by Graham's total disbelief at being told that the crossing point was the same place on both routes.

In spite of our spending many more hours on these routes, which Graham could now walk with ease, he never managed to grasp their true relationship to one another. He believed that what I said was true, and he knew that I had no wish to mislead him, but he still could not imagine the routes in their correct relationship to one another. He eventually conceded that I had to be correct because he never found features identical to those at the crossing point anywhere else on either of the routes. Even taking his finger over a correctly drawn tactile map of the route failed to convince him that my map was any better a representation of the routes than his was, and he accepted them both as equivalent because they both led from A to B.

Congenitally blind people may therefore present problems to the rehabilitation worker when teaching orientation because they conceive of the world differently from sighted people. Traditionally, educators have concentrated on teaching the names of bodily parts in the firm faith that this is necessary for the development of spatial abilities (see, for example, Cratty and Sams, 1968). I have never personally seen the logic in such an argument, and I was relieved to read recently that there appears to be no relationship between the ability to name body parts and orientation ability (Spencer, Blades and Morsley, 1989). The authors more sensibly place an emphasis on real-life experience, fostered through structured play which motivates children and presents them with spatial problems to solve.

Another approach which I would advocate is to devise a number of spatial tasks which the child is required to carry out, beginning with being able to make simple turns in order to retrieve an object within reach; then walking a few paces towards various auditory targets, through to being able to keep track of his changing position in the environment. If a child fails at the simplest level, then they must be taught to a level of competence necessary for success at the next level. By developing a logical sequence of spatial behaviours which can form an orientation ability checklist, O & M teachers can objectively assess performance and improvements resulting from their teaching as well as being able to diagnose where any spatial problems lie.

AIDS TO SPATIAL UNDERSTANDING

Audible maps

Audible maps, at their simplest, are nothing other than stored representations in memory of a series of route instructions. By means of repeating the remembered instructions to himself, the blind traveller can navigate the environment provided he keeps track of where he is and does not forget any of the route information. As routes get longer, however, the probability of forgetting a piece of information or of introducing an error into recall increases. In recognition of this, some workers make use of hand-held memos into which they can dictate the set of route instructions and play them back as they require them.

Audible maps have their uses, but their limitations need to be recognized, both in terms of how much spatial layout information can be obtained from them and the fact that two separate sets of instructions are needed: one for the outward journey and another for the return. This makes audible maps less than optimal when detailed spatial information is to be presented in an economical fashion, and for this reason, other forms of map have been developed.

sublock
celsoms

The bead map

A string of beads with a unique shape of bead representing a distinct route instruction was developed as a one-off aid to orientation by a mobility instructor whose name has long since vanished into the mists of time. Given that it has been around for longer than the auditory map, perhaps the auditory map should be considered as the analogue of the bead map. Both forms of representation assume that successful travel involves the literal carrying out of a finite number of operations specified by an agreed code. Each provides an *algorithm*, that is to say a set of instructions which, if followed correctly, will guarantee success. However, by virtue of their being algorithmic, both bead and auditory maps require a different set of instructions for the return journey, and neither of them can help the traveller re-orientate should he make a wrong turn.

Tactile maps

For some two decades now, systematic raised diagrams and maps have been available to blind people. In the early 1970s, for example, the Blind Mobility Research Unit at the University of Nottingham developed a standardized kit for producing tactile maps via Thermoform technology (Armstrong, 1973). Although the Nottingham Maps Kit is no longer available commercially, the Euro-Town Kit, which incorporates many of the original Nottingham symbols, is available from Marburg (RNIB in the UK). Tactile maps of a high quality are essential for educational purposes, but less high quality maps can be very useful in mobility lessons.

A recent development which has taken place in mapping research is that of the tactile strip map, an idea which has been around for decades but which has only now received proper attention (Golledge, 1991). Tactile strip maps capitalize on the fact that Braille machines use half-inch wide strips of paper which can be rolled up. Onto this strip of paper can be embossed a variety of symbols in linear order. Left and right turns, road crossings and salient landmarks can be embossed in the order in which the traveller will encounter them, and as the strip map is unrolled in the pocket, so the traveller can inconspicuously keep track of his position with respect to the route.

Tactile strip maps are an analogue of audible route maps. The serial order of landmarks is represented, but their true spatial location is not. Unlike audible maps, however, the traveller requires only one map for both outward and return journeys, and this represents an economy in information presentation. They are also less dependent upon technology for their use, and it is surprising that they have only received such recent attention, given that their true precursor, the bead map, has been around for so long.

Audible compass

Sighted travellers use compasses in order to help them navigate over large distances where the destination and origin of the route cannot be simultaneously perceived. A Braille version of a sighted compass, known as the Silva compass, has been available for many years, but it needs to be held level in order to function properly, and this is not easily achievable without sight. In order to inform a blind traveller of the changes in direction he makes as he moves through the environment, Yngstrom (1989) developed an audible compass which is attached to a belt worn around the waist. Such an idea is based on a prototype produced at the Blind Mobility Research Unit which was found to be useful in rural, but not urban environments. This was due to interference from electromagnets in dynamos and starter motors fitted to parked vehicles.

The rationale for an audible compass worn round the waist was that it leaves the hands free and can give continuous orientation information. The user can preselect a direction on the compass by turning a knob. When he is facing in that direction an audible tone ceases to sound, thereby keeping him on course. Deviations left and right from the set course produce a tone which can be cancelled by means of the appropriate change of direction. Such a device should be used as an orientation teaching device with all congenitally blind children, to give them the feedback from movement with respect to the environment which they otherwise lack. This would help them to develop an external frame of reference for movement and discourge egocentric spatial coding strategies.

NOMAD

The most recent and exciting development in the field of tactile mapping is the audio-tactile mapping and graphics tool called NOMAD (Dodds, 1988b; Parkes, 1988). NOMAD is named after an Australian guide dog with whose owner the inventor was acquainted. NOMAD is a device of immense potential, but its main advantage over existing tactile graphics is that it removes the Braille labels which tend to clutter up the map, and places the information formerly carried by them on software which is dedicated to each graphic and which produces its output via a speech-synthesizer. By means of a touch-sensitive pad beneath the current graphic, NOMAD senses the position of the user's finger on the graphic and speaks the message appropriate to that point on the map.

Users can also create their own library of graphics and can edit a graphic in order to delete or to replace a given piece of information. NOMAD can also take the user round a graphic. By specifying a location, for example, NOMAD can direct the user's finger down, up, left and right until the required destination is reached, whereupon it will speak the name of that location. Many other facilities, too numerous to mention here, are available, and it is to be hoped that by the end of the century more congenitally blind children will have had the opportunity to learn about geography and spatial layout on such a machine. NOMAD is compatible with IBM and Apple Macintosh IIG micro-computers, and its current cost is in the region of £1 000. This price includes a Dolphin Apollo synthesizer and a capacity to work in eight languages, including Japanese using Japanese DOS and a Sanyo sythesizer.

WHICH IS BEST?

Most rehabilitation workers and mobility specialists simply want to know which method is best for any particular child or adult. Given the apparently universal finding that total congenital blindness does present the individual with problems in understanding environmental layout and orientation with respect to a spatial frame of reference, one would conclude that audible and tactile strip maps would be of greatest benefit for the purposes of navigation.

To assert this does not mean that euclidean maps are not suitable for congenitally blind people; it does suggest, however that the true spatial relationships represented on a euclidean map may not be utilized by the individual. Routes, however, can be derived from systematic exploration of euclidean maps, but research has yet to determine how much additional information the congenitally blind person can store and manipulate.

With the advent of new technology such as NOMAD, perhaps we will witness a quantum leap in the congenitally blind person's understanding of spatial relations over the next few decades. Conventional tactile maps and graphics are so cluttered with labels that the spatial information is being constantly interfered with at the perceptual level. Recognizing this helps us to understand how the information may be stored incorrectly, or how irrelevant boundaries to areas provided by labels may impede the understanding of the spatial information present.

Whereas the eye can take in at a glance what is relevant and what is not, the fingers of the hand are forced to explore a map sequentially over time, with many intervening movements of the hand taking place. Keeping track of these movements is a task in itself, as is the reading of tactile labels which may initially appear to be part of the spatial configuration. Separating out the what from the where as NOMAD does, should vastly simplify the pick-up of spatial information presented to touch.

Before concluding our exploration of congenital blindness perhaps we should consider how congenitally blind people construe our sighted world. We seem to think that sight is such a wonderful sense that those who have never had it must in some way suffer from this lost channel of information and communication. Yet, in my experience, this is not so. Congenitally blind people are sometimes reluctant to talk about the sighted world, partly because to do so places them at an apparent disadvantage. They may have gaps in their knowledge which are of little consequence to them, so that they may not understand what a cloud formation is, or what shadows are, except by means of analogy to their auditory or tactile experience. But they may not share our view about how useful sight is, and we should never assume that they do.

As a real-life anecdote, consider the case of the blind youth whose sighted friend takes him out for a drink during the school vacation. On the way to the pub, the sighted friend remarks that it is a full moon. His blind friend replies that he knows this too, because he read it in the newspaper through his Kurtzweil reading machine. 'But do you know where the moon is?' asks his friend. 'Somewhere up there', he replies, pointing vaguely above his head. His friend corrects him in the direction of his pointing, and they continue along the road, discussing how things change their position as one moves with respect to them.

Several minutes later, they enter a public house, go upstairs and order some drinks. Later in the evening, the blind friend, who had obvioulsy been pondering on the moon question, asks his friend where the moon is now. As the sighted friend can no longer see the moon because they are indoors and the curtains are pulled, he is unable to say. 'Well', said his blind friend, 'I don't think much of sight if it's that unreliable'. His friend is temporarily silenced by this remark, but recovers his composure by asking him, 'Well then, what would you like to have?' The reply is as surprising as it is immediate: 'Much longer arms!'

So far we have considered a number of aspects of congenital blindness in terms of how the individual experiences and stores environmental information. Those of you who have travelled extensively under blindfold during your training will recall how the world seemed to be comprised of a series of sounds which presented themselves to the ears from various directions in a predictable order. Given that there is an auditory representation in the blind traveller's head it is surprising that no-one has thought of devising a binaural recording of a route to see if that helps the individual navigate it better after listening to it.

Perhaps sighted people are so hide-bound by their visual ideas of maps that this possibility has not been explored sufficiently. Even the term 'auditory map' begs the question that the representation has to be like a visual map. I suspect that temporal elements are much more important in the environmental representation of blind travellers than are spatial ones. Let us hope that researchers will continue to investigate these possibilities. Meanwhile, as practitioners, we should constantly strive to develop systematic ways of assessing our clients' spatial skills and evaluating any changes in them resulting from our interventions. If we do not, then in decades to come we will still not have a sufficient understanding of spatial abilities to help those congenitally blind people whose way of dealing with environmental layout may be different from our own.

Important as spatial representation is, we must not forget that congenitally blind people may have rehabilitation requirements of which orientation and mobility training represent only a small part. Some congenitally blind adults present in their middle years for independent living skill training because their parents, by whom they may have been over-protected for decades, are no longer alive or fit enough to be able to look after them. In the case of Graham O., for example, because he had never been allowed to have money in his possession and had been formally educated before decimalization took place in the early 1970s, he had to be taught how to deal with the 'new' currency.

In this chapter we have examined a number of issues surrounding total congenital blindness, and we have seen that genuine difficulties can be observed in people who have never been able to experience the totality of the environment. The need to carry out systematic tests of the individual's spatial understanding cannot be over-emphasized, and the use of tactile maps should not be precluded automatically, even if it takes considerable ingenuity in conveying the conventions of mapping. Also, one must not make the mistake of assuming that all sighted concepts can be translated directly into the experience of the congenitally blind person. Those of you who are interested in concept development in blind children should consult Best (1992) and Hill and Blasch, (1980).

Lastly, it should be recognized that congenitally blind people may simply have an incomplete understanding of certain aspects of the world because they cannot experience them directly, and that part of your job is to assess the degree to which they attribute the same meaning as you do to words which may have a predominantly or even a uniquely visual referent. Never take it for granted that the congenitally blind person's use of language corresponds to yours and take time to let the client experience as much of the situation as possible, using scale models if this should not prove feasible. Above all, never stop asking yourself how you might go about teaching the task differently and be prepared to learn when your client violates any naive assumptions that you might unwittingly make.

8

Anxiety, stress and the learning process

Chapter 3 demonstrated how anxiety and depression are common features of the emotional consequences of sight loss, and an alternative account of depression to that offered by the loss model has been examined. Whereas depression is characterized by a low level of arousal, anxiety is regarded by some psychologists as over-arousal, and over-arousal is perceived to be part of the response to psychological stress. Stress can mean different things to different people, but the most common responses people give when asked what stress means to them are feelings of pressure, either emotional or at work, and of feeling tired, irritable and unable to cope. These answers fall into two categories: first, those relating to the *cause* of stress; second, those relating to the *effects* of stress.

Stress can therefore be seen to follow the recognition that the demands being made upon the individual exceed his ability to rise to them, and this recognition produces an increase in arousal or anxiety that the person can cope. Recent thinking recognizes that stress can be thought of as consisting of two types of arousal. The first is *somatic*, or bodily arousal, and this can be felt as tension in the head, tightness in the stomach, increased tremor in the hands, sweating and so on. The second type of arousal is *cognitive*, or mental arousal, and its effects can be manifested in an inability to concentrate, poor attention, difficulty in recalling things, the intrusion of obsessional thoughts which cannot be stopped, or even flashbacks, a common feature of post-traumatic stress disorder.

Although somatic anxiety and cognitive arousal are conceptually distinct, in practice they tend to go together, so that it is common for clients to exhibit symptoms of both simultaneously. When questioned about their levels of arousal, many people are genuinely unable to say just how they feel, and may have to be presented with statements about their somatic and cognitive states before they can be made aware of them. Spielberger, Vagg, Barker *et al.* (1980) conceptualize anxiety as being either a personality trait or a fleeting state. This recognizes that there are individuals whom we can regard as characteristically anxious, but that even people who are not normally anxious can show anxiety in certain situations.

COPING AND STRESS

How a person behaves can have a direct effect on how well they can cope with stress. Lazarus (1966) has looked at what has become to be known as 'coping style', which is an abstract way of looking at a variety of behaviours in which the person may engage in an attempt to reduce their stress. Three main types of coping have been identified. The first is what is known as emotion-focused coping. Emotion-focused ways of coping commonly used are relaxation techniques such as breathing exercises; listening to tapes; meditating and self-talk. The second is known as problem-focused coping. Problem-focused coping is characterized by the individual engaging in task-centred behaviour such as getting information about being blind; getting some independence skills, and so on. The third type of coping is known as avoidance coping. This is characterized by the individual day-dreaming, denying that they have a problem, putting off doing anything at all, or escaping from the situation by means of alcohol or drugs.

Although three main categories of coping behaviour have been identified, an individual may engage in all three to some extent. Which form dominates, however, determines the coping style. In terms of the most adaptive form of coping, problem-focused coping is clearly what is going to succeed in the long term, although emotion-focused coping may be the next best bet if the problem cannot be resolved satisfactorily. Such are the implications of sight loss that all of its consequences are unlikely to be perceived at once, and stress is likely to be experienced repeatedly as each new implication dawns and as new frustrations present themselves. The ability of the individual to recruit the range of coping responses is likely to be the best predictor of final outcome.

It is important to recognize that avoidance and emotion-focused coping, although perhaps understandable in the early stages of reaction to sight loss, should eventually be replaced by something more positive. It is part of your job as rehabilitation worker to help foster positive coping in your client by confronting him with the reality of his problems and offering him a variety of means of solving them. Clients who are receiving rehabilitation at a residential centre are more easily able to receive appropriate (and sometimes inappropriate!) emotional support from other clients than is a client who remains in the context of the family, where support can so easily foster dependency.

Although individuals may have coping styles which have been adaptive in their previous, sighted lives, the loss of sight may prevent them from using them. Certainly, the early stages when the individual has not yet learned alternative ways of tackling things, practical coping behaviours may simply not be present, only avoidant or emotion-focused ones. Traditional avoidant coping behaviours, such as reading escapist literature, or watching soap operas on television, may no longer be possible, and new avoidant behaviours may develop, such as blotting out all feeling by means of recourse to alcohol.

As you impart independence skills, so you give your client a range of ways of dealing with demands which were not present before. What needs to be recognized is that even simple tasks can present apparently insurmountable hurdles to the client, so that stress is experienced at almost every level where some form of activity is required. It is therefore important to recognize that your client may not be able to cope with excessive task demands at the beginning of training because he finds everything too stressful, and that more stresses are likely to arise as he develops skills which will inevitably place him in progressively more threatening situations.

The most useful message that the rehabilitation worker can give the client is that she has encountered people who have felt exactly the same as they do, and that the distress experienced is quite normal under the circumstances. Following this message should come the intimation that if the client trusts the rehabilitation worker's judgment, then these thoughts and feelings will change and the client will feel that he can cope with life once again. In the following sections we shall look at the ways in which you can help your clients to solve their current problems in a framework of theories of motivation. These theories are basically simple and really only common sense, although the language in which they are couched may appear somewhat pretentious. However, the principles are sound and they have been shown to work in a variety of settings (Dodds, 1989; Schunk, 1984).

SELF-EFFICACY THEORY

In Chapter 3 the relationship between depression and learned helplessness was examined. The opposite of feeling helpless is that of feeling efficacious, and Bandura's (1977) theory of self-efficacy in relation to self-esteem and depression was looked at. When we feel efficacious we cannot wait to start something and we look forward to the activity in itself as well as the anticipated success of its outcome. In addition, if we feel high in self-efficacy our mood is also likely to be buoyant. Thus self-efficacy has behavioural, cognitive and emotional components. No wonder it is such a powerful motivating force, determining whether we sit around feeling gloomy and not bothering to try something, or whether we throw ourselves whole-heartedly into an activity, expecting success.

According to self-efficacy theory, self-efficacy information comes from a number of different sources, and it is possible to identify as many as six of these. The first is directly from one's performance at a given task. If one is successful, then one's self-efficacy increases; if one fails, then one's sense of self-efficacy decreases. The second is from verbal comments made by the teacher: praise increases self-efficacy, criticism lowers it. The third comes from social feedback on our performance: approval from onlookers or significant others increases self-efficacy; disapproval from peers, or the message that we could have done better, lowers it.

The fourth source of self-efficacy comes from an awareness of one's own physiological state immediately before carrying out a task. Tenseness in the stomach, clammy hands, and so on signal that not all is well, and these signs of anxiety tell us that we are not really performing confidently. The fifth source of self-efficacy comes from the presence of positive role models with whom we can identify. When we see someone in similar circumstances successfully carrying out a task which we will be expected to do, we feel that we ourselves stand a decent chance of succeeding at that task. Finally, the ways in which we attribute success or failure to ourselves, to chance or to circumstances beyond our control can affect not only our self-efficacy, but also our self-esteem, as demonstrated in Chapter 3.

Self-efficacy theory has been highly successful in motivating children in the classroom (Schunk, 1984), increasing their self-esteem and improving the performance of those who expect to fail, and its principles can be employed equally successfully in one-to-one teaching. Before going on to elaborate the numerous ways in which self-efficacy may be increased, let us examine briefly several other important factors involved in learning, namely goal-setting, feedback, knowledge of results and contingency, because they are all closely linked with the development of self-efficacy and can help us to understand that notoriously vague term 'motivation' in ways which enable us to have a direct effect upon it. Indeed, since workers such as Welsh (1986) have identified that client motivation is cited as the most important cause of failure of rehabilitation, any greater understanding of this aspect of learning can only improve our effectiveness as rehabilitation workers.

GOAL-SETTING THEORY

Goal-setting research has been carried out in industry, in education and in clinical practice. Locke and Latham (1984) identified four reasons why goal-setting can affect performance. The first is that goals direct attention and action; the second is that goals mobilize and regulate the amount of effort people are prepared to put into a task; the third is that goals can produce persistence; and the fourth is that goals can motivate people to develop alternative ways or strategies of achieving them. There is however, a fifth way in which goal-setting can affect performance, namely through its influence on levels of anxiety, and this is something which needs to be kept in mind throughout the client's rehabilitation.

Goal-setting is something in which all rehabilitation workers must be engaged however conscious or otherwise they may be of this. It is important, therefore, to recognize that goal-setting can be done on the basis of well-worked out principles. In the first place, goals can be regarded as long-term or short-term. For example, the long-term goal is to get the client to become independent. This term is necessarily vague, and the ultimate goal is very distant. However distant, global goals break down into more immediate, specific ones, such as sighted guide or diagonal cane technique, personal care skills and communication via Braille, Moon, magnified print or the use of high technology such as the micro-computer with speech synthesis.

Research has shown that by setting your client short-term, attainable goals you will stand a much better chance of him becoming independent than if you go for vague, long-term goals (Bandura and Schunk, 1981). This is known as goal proximity. However, setting short-term, attainable goals crucially depends upon your having made an accurate assessment of your client's capabilities. You must make sure that the goals you set are in fact attainable by the client, and not allow him to fail: in other words, your goals must be realistic and set in the context of the client's current abilities and skill level, as well as his current aspirations.

In addition, we must recognize the difference between goals which you assign to your client and those which you negotiate with him. Research has shown that adults show a great commitment to goals in whose setting they themselves have participated than those to which they have been assigned by someone else (Tubbs, 1986). In the early stages of learning, assigned goals are bound to predominate, but in the later stages, when goals become less specific and more distant, allowing your clients to choose from a number of alternatives is likely to increase their motivation and persistence in the face of adversity.

TASK ANALYSIS

The best way of implementing goal-setting principles is by undertaking what is known as a task analysis before beginning to teach the new skill. Task analysis is not a new thing; it has been around at least since the days of Henry Ford and mass production in industry, but its relevance to rehabilitation has perhaps not been fully appreciated. To those of you who are already implementing task analysis without perhaps realizing it, a brief description will soon make it recognizable. To those who are not, it offers a better way of going about things than an intuitive one which, although it may work much of the time, can often fail with certain clients.

A task analysis of blind mobility led successfully to the development of the long-cane system as we know it today. Walking about could be seen to be composed of a number of distinct tasks, each of which could be identified as having a specific set of skills associated with it. For example, stopping in time at a down-kerb requires the traveller to have a small amount of fore-warning of the impending change in surface level. The problem facing those who wanted to make mobility available to those without sufficient sight was to develop a tactile means of achieving the same end, which the cane does admirably.

In spite of the success of task analysis in explicating the requirements for safe travel, no-one appears to have considered the need to carry out task analyses of activities of daily living, such as self-care and communication with others. Perhaps it is because mobility is simply the same set of problems recurring regularly at each step that it has given up its secrets so readily to task analysis. Yet one could argue the case for a similar amount of research effort being put into other aspects of independent living, particularly where new ways of dealing with familiar objects is concerned, or when new devices and techniques have to be mastered.

In the absence of this having been carried out, I would like to suggest that, whatever task you are teaching, you try to break it down into its component parts so that the perceptual and motor requirements of these components become obvious. It is only by doing this that you will be able to assess with any degree of accuracy how likely your client is going to be able to cope with the various task components and their associated skills, and by what means. In order to clarify this point, let us take an apparently simple independent living skill such as filling a kettle, which is just one sub-task within the overall task of making a cup of tea.

When we examine the task closely, we find that it can be decomposed into a further number of even smaller tasks. This is illustrated in Figure 8.1. In the example under considera- tion, each operation in the sequence demands a certain level

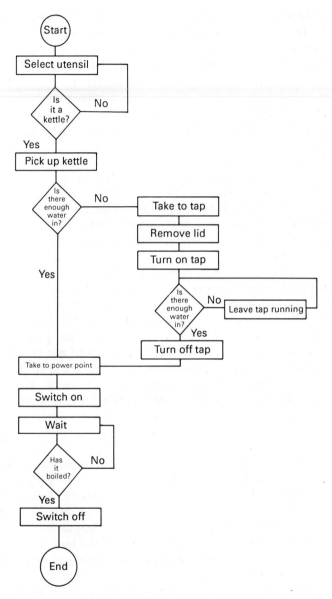

Figure 8.1 Flow diagram for filling a kettle.

of competence in order for it to be carried out reliably and safely. In normal circumstances, the sub-tasks would be carried out visually, but they can be carried out by other means. By looking at the operations required at the various stages in the task, it will become clear what these alternative means need to be.

A flow diagram such as the one above could easily form the basis for a computer programme for a robot which could perform the activity of filling a kettle. By setting out the sequence of operations in this way, it becomes apparent that before moving on to the next stage in the task, the system (in our case, the client) needs to have feedback from its actions. For example, it needs to know if it has succeeded in achieving each goal. If it has not, then it has to act again until it has. Only when each condition has been satisfied can it move on the next one.

For those of you who may think that the flow chart is simply stating the obvious, consider for a moment what sort of sensory and motor requirements would be needed in order to carry out the various checks. A specification even at this level would provide a robotics engineer with many headaches, particularly if it was specified to him that the robot would not be able to utilize the equivalent of 'visual' information. For example, we know that whereas a sighted person can see at a glance whether or not the kettle is sufficiently filled, the visually impaired person may not be able to judge this so easily. We also know that the changing sound of the water going in can serve as one cue, as can the increasing weight of the kettle. But these are complex skills which have to be learned as they are not habitual ways of making that particular judgment.

In addition, the activities required in order to achieve the end point in the sequence may themselves be difficult for the client to perform, perhaps because of an impairment in the visual identification of the components of the task, the visual control of the movements required at various stages of the task, or through a physical limitation on the movements imposed by an additional disability. Even a minor weakness in a limb resulting from a stroke can render an otherwise simple task difficult, necessitating a further analysis of how the task could possibly be carried out. Often a task is rendered difficult or impossible to execute by perhaps just one small problem at a crucial point, such as the inability to hold the now full kettle because of its weight.

Depending on your client's current level of sensory and physical functioning, certain aspects of the overall task may obviously present problems whereas others may not. For example, visual acuity may be adequate for identifying the cup, saucer and teaspoon, but may not be adequate to monitor the rise of level of the liquid inside the cup. Improving the lighting or contrast of the situation may solve the problem, but again it may not. If it does not, then the need for a liquid level indicator is made obvious. But if any single sub-task cannot be carried out with complete confidence, then the overall task will not have been mastered successfully. Only by means of task analysis will you be able to identify accurately in advance what problems to expect, and be able to decide how these problems can then be solved.

FEEDBACK, KNOWLEDGE OF RESULTS AND CONTINGENCY

Feedback was examined above in connection with self-efficacy. Another term for feedback is knowledge of results, and knowledge of results has long been known to improve performance on motor tasks. Effectively, you provide your client with feedback every time you make a comment on his technique. Feedback provides the learner with two sorts of information. First, it informs him of the magnitude of his error, such as the degree to which his cane is off-centre. Second, it can motivate him and affect his persistence, for example via a comment such as 'Good, only a few more paces to go and we're there', or 'That's the way; you're beginning to get the hang of the gadget now'.

The reason why some clients find learning difficult is that they are used to visual feedback immediately informing them of the consequences of their own actions. Without vision, you have to be their eyes in this respect. Feedback has to follow some aspect of your client's behaviour, but it is not to be confused with providing a running commentary on what is happening around him. Often, feedback can be used to stop the client at the end of one sub-task before he goes on to the next one. A simple, 'OK. That's good', combined with a gentle hand on the client's arm can serve to stop him from going beyond his capabilities and failing at the next stage. Clients can become over-confident and attempt things which they have not yet been taught, and it is your job to control the pace of learning so that more successes than failures are experienced.

Feedback following on from behaviour is known as con-tingency, and it is a powerful feature of good teaching (Wood, Wood and Middleton, 1978). It can take a number of forms, the simplest being verbal praise for having attained a goal, and you will give your client praise many times during a lesson. However, contingent teaching does not simply consist of giving verbal feedback. If a client should fail to experience success at a particular goal, then a contingent teacher will immediately set a slightly less difficult goal or one which does not require the action which the client failed to produce. If the client should succeed, the contingent teacher will go on to set a slightly more difficult task.

By structuring the task and breaking it down into its components, the teacher can ensure that the client experiences successes most of the time. However, not all clients become demoralized by the odd failure, and some are able to laugh it off and benefit from their occasional mistakes. As someone once said, there is no such thing as failure: only feedback. Yet some people never seem to benefit from feedback, and it remains a curious enigma even to the psychologist when little learning appears to be taking place in spite of the teacher engineering clear and simple situations with careful attention to details. In such cases one must assume that the client's attention has somehow not been engaged adequately, and the relevance of the current activity to his overall aspirations may need to be checked out.

In addition to being contingent, the instructor can also take care of the client's motivational state by ensuring that when failure does occur, he is never allowed to attribute this to his own incompetence, carelessness or lack of effort. It is easy to praise the client for trying but not succeeding, and to take the responsibility for any failures oneself. Just apologise and explain that you were asking too much of him at this stage. Motivation is often a fragile commodity and if the client is to remain well-motivated you must engineer things so that feel-ings of and attributions for success remain within him. Never try to take credit for your client's successes, even although you may be helping him out quite a lot of the time. To do so deprives him of the satisfaction of achievement, and it can also make him dependent upon you.

As a number of new terms have been introduced in this chapter, let us briefly recap, in order that we do not forget how they all fit together. Losing one's sight is a stressful experience, and learning new skills places the client under even more pressure. Signs of stress are anxiety or over-arousal, and feelings of failure can be uppermost in the client's mind. Loss of sight means loss of skills, and feelings of helplessness may present. In order to reduce your client's stress and make the acquisition of independence skills relatively painless for him, you need to present the rehabilitation in such a way as to foster a sense of self-efficacy, and this is best achieved by breaking down the overall goal of independence into specific, challenging, realistic, acceptable and measurable goals. If you feel that you might forget these five points, just remember the acronym SCRAM.

By adhering to goal-setting principles you will help yourself as well as your client. Instead of experiencing frustration as your client encounters yet another failure, you will experience exhilaration at how well your client is learning. If you do find that your client is still experiencing failure, then you have to analyse what it is that you are doing wrong. Are you expecting him to have to remember too much? Do you have a communication problem? Is his technique up to the demands placed upon him? Are you giving him the right sort of feedback at the right time?

Used in a systematic way, task analysis can help you set your client goals which are within his grasp, success at which can spur him on to further tasks or to further sub-goals which place the end-point of the overall task within reach. In effect, you will be directly controlling your client's level of motivation, so that you will never need to use the excuse, 'Well, I did what I could, but he just wasn't motivated'. Motivation is something which responds to events going on outside of the head, not just events going on inside it. Also, failures demoralize instructors as much as clients, so that they should be prevented from occurring if both parties are to get any enjoyment from working together.

MORE ADVANCED TECHNIQUES

Once your client has developed the basic independence skills and has acquired some confidence in the system, you can begin to involve him in setting his own goals within your overall lesson plans and also make the goals more long-term. The more your client is personally involved in the lesson the more he is going to learn, and you should take every opportunity of presenting him with novel experiences which are typical of the sort he is going to experience in everyday life. In that way, it is likely that his learning will transfer more easily to other tasks where the same skills are required, rather than being limited to training routes or to specific independent living tasks.

Many people argue that skill learning must be distinguished from learning to solve problems, and the techniques so far described should be regarded as dealing with skill learning rather than problem-solving. But being blind or partially sighted involves the continual solving of problems as new situations are encountered and cues have to be disambiguated, so that you should try to foster the ability to solve problems in your client. One way of doing this is to place your client in a novel situation which has an element of the unexpected in it. This will test your client's assumptions about the world and force him to use all of the information he has to arrive at the right conclusion.

In the previous book, examples were given of two instructional styles in mobility training which could not have looked more different, and they were characterized as the authoritarian style and the egalitarian style (Dodds, 1988a, pp. 73–6). These labels, however, serve more to pass judgment on the instructor than to characterize the ways in which the instruction differs. In the examples given, the authoritarian instructor was sighted, whereas the egalitarian instructor was blind. This suggests that the blind instructor may have to rely on her client telling her what he is experiencing if she is to be able to direct his attention to the appropriate aspects of the task in hand. Perhaps, by virtue of their situation, blind instructors are forced to use egalitarian methods of instruction, whereas sighted instructors, because they can see everything all at once, can be biased towards authoritarian ones.

At the time when I wrote about instructional style, I was not intimately acquainted with instructional theory, and I characterized the blind instructor's style as allowing the client to learn through what I termed 'structured discovery'. This is very different from setting short-term goals with immediate feedback, which is appropriate during the early stages of learning with all clients, and which may be as far as many of your clients are ever going to get. But structured discovery learning, used with clients who are not afraid to be set challenges, can produce levels of self-reliant independence which cannot be surpassed by existing methods. Having now read more in this area, I have discovered that very similar terminology has been used in precisely the same way by a number of learning theorists (Kagan, 1966; Keislar and Shulman, 1966), and hence it has a respectable pedigree.

The basis of structured discovery learning is to place your client in an environment which you know completely, and to structure his experiences in it in such a way as to require him to use all of the information available in order to figure out what is going on. One way of presenting him with a problem is to withhold some vital piece of information which he himself can deduce from other information available to him, and to encourage him to reflect on this information and to put it together to solve the problem. In effect, this is the Socratic method, known as such because Socrates successfully got a slave to prove Pythagoras' Theorem by getting him to reflect on what he already knew.

To take an example of this approach (Dodds, 1985), the blind instructor asks the student (myself under blindfold) to walk a route without telling him that it consists of a cul-de-sac. On arriving at the end of the route, the student has initially no idea that he has ended up almost back at where he started, although he discovers that this appears to be the case after having explored the route another couple of times. Using perceptual cues such as sun or wind direction, the student applies his understanding of how the world is laid out to arrive at the correct conclusion. After a little reflection, the hypothesis that this is indeed the case enters the student's mind, and he then goes off to test it by squaring off and crossing the road. He finds his hypothesis confirmed when he arrives at the opposite up-kerb and encounters a landmark with which he is already familiar.

Getting lost is one of many blind travellers' greatest fears, and I suspect that it is because some instructors are content for their clients to learn routes by rote rather than to engage in active orientation work in their heads. If there is no need to figure out where you are, then you are never going to acquire the skill of orientation, so that in order to foster this ability the instructor must present the client with orientation problems and guide his problem-solving if he is unable initially to do this for himself.

The aim of discovery learning is to develop problem-solving abilities upon which true independence is based. Its goal should be to get the client to ask himself, 'Given that such and such is the experience I am having, what must be the case for the experience to be the way it is?' The correct answer is always a combination of what the environment is like and what the client has done in that environment. A faulty model of the environment is always due to the client misconstruing what he has done, unless someone changes the layout of the world overnight (and this sometimes happens!). By getting your client into the habit of constantly checking the consistency of the information he gathers, you will place him in a position of feeling confident of handling any novel situation, and this, in turn, will keep up his motivation to travel.

Lest anyone should doubt the views expressed here, they would do worse than to visit the Services for the Visually Impaired in Lincoln, Nebraska, where blind instructors are employed and a philosophy of education based on independence acquisition is vigorously pursued. Students who have failed to benefit from traditional methods of sighted instruction often leave the Centre with a degree of independence which astonishes even themselves. Part of this stems from the fact that blind rehabilitation staff provide the most positive role model possible, but other factors are involved.

The Centre is currently developing an explicit philosophy of training based on the idea that adults must have the right attitude towards independence; that they need to assume responsibility for their own learning right from the start; that discovery learning is superior to guided instruction; and that traditional training methods have tended to have a low impact on the student population. One of the perceived main deficiencies of much of existing training is a tendency to emphasize task-specific solutions at the expense of devoting adequate effort to teaching how these solutions may be transferable to new problems (Mettler, 1990; Roberts, 1990).

In this chapter we have covered a wide range of material, and the reader may be wondering how, if ever, she can implement all of the suggestions offered here. The answer is simple: take on board maybe just one or two techniques to start with; for example, goal-setting and task-analysis, and see how you get on with them. Try to keep accurate records of your teaching and compare your results using the new techniques with previous results. Then move on to try another one or two, such as the structured discovery learning and problem-solving.

In order to maximize the chances of success for yourself, choose a suitable client, so that you do not risk undermining their confidence or subjecting them to too much stress. Whereas goal-setting reduces stress, discovery learning may increase it. Recognize that you may have to plan your lessons more carefully now that you are becoming more aware of their structure, and that this all takes up additional time. Above all, if you feel that you are doing fine as you are, then stick with that. If you were that bad you would be the first to know about it – wouldn't you?

9

Low vision

THE ROOT OF THE PROBLEM

One of the most taxing aspects of rehabilitation is the initial assessment of residual visual functioning in the client who has some degree of vision left. First of all, it is important to establish whether the visual problem lies solely within the eye, or whether it stems from some more central problem within the brain. We have looked in some detail at the effects of brain damage on visual perception, but the majority of clients will simply have something wrong with their eyes, and the remainder of their visual system is unlikely to be affected.

Although we have seen that the eye-as-camera approach to the understanding of visual perception is unhelpful at best and misleading at worst, at the level of the formation of the retinal image it is a highly appropriate analogy, as it helps us to understand how the information contained in the optic array is transmitted to the receptor surface. In the normal eye, the textural gradients which specify a continuous path, the expansion patterns which specify hit or miss paths of objects ahead, and the shearing of textural elements which specifies the relative motion of surfaces with respect to one another are all faithfully reproduced in miniature on the surface of the retina due to the convergence of light rays produced by the lens.

In the case of an eye which lacks acuity, and a large number of clients will suffer from this problem, the resolution of this fine detail is lost, and this has important consequences for visual perception. To take an obvious example, the continuousness or otherwise of a surface can no longer be directly perceived as the slight textural differences within and between surfaces are undetectable. So that a pavement and a road may no longer be seen to be separated by a kerb. In mobility terms, this is disastrous, as a step which is planned to take place on a continuous surface ends up taking place between two discontinuous surfaces, to the detriment of confident travel.

Another common consequence of this loss of information is that the expansion patterns which normally specify hit or miss paths are absent. In terms of the control of movement, these are serious deficits which can affect almost every action the person tries to perform, whether this is walking around an obstacle or bringing a cup towards the mouth. Let us consider these two cases for a moment, because although the two tasks look entirely different on the surface, on closer analysis they can be seen to involve the same principles.

In each case, expansion patterns in the optic array specify not only collision paths, they specify the time to collision: if the same rate and direction of change is maintained, then the object will strike the body at a specified point. Whether this occurs or not can be determined in two ways. First, the nature of the expansion pattern can be altered by changing the movements which produce it. In the case of bodily movement in relation to an obstacle, the next step can cause the body to veer, changing the position of the expansion node in the optic array so that it specifies a miss rather than a hit. Second, in the case of the cup approaching the mouth, the rate of approach can be monitored to ensure that there is deceleration towards the end of the movement. If the eye lacks the ability to resolve this information then the brain cannot take care of it automatically, and conscious strategies need to be learned in order to compensate for this.

One of the most common consequences of loss of visual acuity is that distances between parts of the body or between the body and objects around it cannot be judged accurately. We are seldom required to make absolute distance judgments, but distances relative to the body need to be judged continually over a wide range of situations. This is because we constantly move towards or away from objects around us, or we move them towards or away from our bodies. Because movements have a beginning and an end, we need to be able to increase and decrease their speed during the course of the movement. Since speed is defined in terms of distance over time, if distance cannot be estimated accurately, then neither can speed. And if speed cannot be estimated accurately, then it cannot be controlled properly. In practical terms, this means that visual control of any movement at all becomes unreliable, resulting in errors and accidents.

These various losses of information are often compounded for the low vision client, but the basic causes of his difficulties are wholly attributable to the failure of the eye to extract the detailed information in the optic array which is necessary for the automatic control of movements appropriate to the situation. Outdoors the traveller may find himself unsure of where to place his foot next, how close an approaching object may be, or how near to the kerb edge he is. Indoors he may fail to notice when a cupboard door is left open as the textural shearing which would normally specify such a situation is no longer available to an eye which has a reduced acuity. The net result of this loss of information is that the client becomes unsure of himself when making any sort of movement at all, and the loss of confidence in his vision may make him reluctant to persevere with his remaining sight.

In the case of the visual control of arm movements, the expansion pattern which specifies that the cup is on target for the mouth may be absent, resulting in a miss. Accidents such as these can easily destroy a person's confidence in their residual sight and make it difficult for the rehabilitation worker to persuade the client that his remaining vision can be useful. In such cases assessments should be made at every level on as wide a range of independence tasks as possible, and under a variety of lighting levels ranging from bright sunlight, through artificial domestic illumination, to outdoor, night-time environments. In this way, a coherent picture of which the client can or cannot do reliably with vision will emerge, and strategies of remediation will become obvious, given sufficient imagination and ingenuity on the part of the rehabilitation worker, and motivation to persevere on the part of the client.

Some people who lose so much of their sight that they cannot make out faces, objects or any feature at all of their environment give up completely on residual vision which could serve them usefully during mobility by giving them some clue as to their orientation. The direction of the sun outdoors, or the position of a window indoors can be perceived by people with little more than light perception. This information is useful, and clients should be encouraged to look for such visual cues, no matter how poor or inadequate they may appear to them (Freeman and Jose, 1992; Jose, 1983).

SIMULATION OF LOW VISION

Although it is easy to simulate total blindness by donning a sleepshade, it is not so easy to simulate a wide number of eye conditions producing low vision. This is because we can only introduce some impediment to light rays reaching our retinas by means of placing something in front of our own, normal eyes. So that a whole host of perceptual problems caused by structural defects in the eye cannot be simulated accurately. Even tunnel vision cannot be simulated as we see a sharp, black edge at the onset of the tunnel which the tunnel vision sufferer does not see, and macular degeneration is completely impossible to simulate with any accuracy without wearing special contact lenses.

People who experience low vision will often say that the world appears to lie behind a frosted glass, such as a steamed up bathroom window. Others will report a haze which appears to float and even shimmer in front of everything they look at. Some clients will have been totally unaware of defects such as field losses until you put them through your assessment. It is not uncommon for a client to be unaware of the fact that he is totally blind in one eye because the field loss experienced is very small. Hemianopias are often only noticed when the client starts bumping into things on one side, although he may not attribute this to a sight defect.

THE EXPERIENCE OF LOW VISION

Certain conditions which produce low vision can be perceptually infuriating. Distorted vision can result from a fold in the surface of a retina which has become detached but reattached imperfectly. To the sufferer, the world looks like a Cubist painting where the spatial elements of the scene are not preserved. The problem is aggravated if the defect lies in the dominant eye, in which case the only 'cure' is to wear a frosted glass in the lens, which some people may refuse to do on the grounds that it is cosmetically unacceptable to them.

Double vision (diplopia) is another particularly distressing phenomenon, and one which can develop for a variety of reasons. In many cases, it is a relatively simple problem which is correctable, and a client reporting double vision should be referred to an optometrist, who can prescribe a prism to restore binocular vision. However, double vision can also be caused by a problem in the brain, and if there are additional symptoms such as headache or nausea, the client should be referred via their general practitioner to a neurologist, particularly if they have recently suffered a fall or lost consciousness.

If double vision cannot be corrected, then again it may better for the sufferer to wear a frosted lens over the offending eye and to lose binocular vision than to retain vision in two eyes which do not agree. Binocular vision is not essential for depth perception, although it does assist distance estimation in close-up tasks, and people with monocular vision are able to carry out quite complex tasks such as driving a car without noticeable deterioration in their performance. This is because parallax cues can be produced by means of small, sideways movements of the head.

Residual vision can also introduce into perception distracting visual phenomena such as flashing lights, floaters and the perception of movement which is purely illusory. Like tinnitus to the deaf person, these visual disturbances are distressing and interfere with current task performance because they capture the person's attention. Additionally, the low vision client may experience fluctuations in his sight due to changes in his underlying bodily state, as in the case of diabetes. Clients may have good and bad days, and you will need to get a feel for this if you are to be sensitive in setting realistic goals for your client.

We know that the retinal receptors in our eyes are of two types and that their distribution over the retina differs. The dense clustering of cones in the macula enables us to discriminate fine detail in the centre of the visual field, while the less dense distribution of rods in the remainder of the retina enables us to be aware of small movements in the periphery of the visual field. Certain eye diseases or disorders selectively impair one or other of these functions. Macular degeneration, a common cause of loss of detailed vision in the elderly, affects reading, face perception and the viewing of television, while leaving mobility generally intact. One form of retinitis pigmentosa, on the other hand, can produce the very opposite pattern of deficit, rendering the person incapable of safe mobility while allowing them to enjoy the reading of print.

FIELD DEFECTS

In the normal eye, there is a continuous field of almost 180 degrees, apart from the blind spot, whose presence goes completely unnoticed unless you are playing one of those little games where you have to fixate on a spot, whereupon a letter X positioned an inch or two to the side of it disappears as you do so. Why do we not perceive a hole in the visual field caused by the blind spot? The answer is simple: because there is no information in the optic array to specify the existence of such a hole, we do not perceive the blind spot as a hole which moves around the world as we move our eyes.

Field defects can arise as a result of damage to the receptor cells in the retina, damage to the primary visual analyser in the occipital cortex, or damage to the parietal region of the right hemisphere. In some cases the scotoma can encroach into the macular area, and this affects reading and the identification of objects by their features. Clients suffering from scotomata which impair their vision need to be encouraged or taught to use new fixation strategies whereby they learn to inhibit their automatic eye movements and adopt eccentric (off-centre) fixation (Backman and Inde, 1979; Cummings, Whittacker, Watson *et al.*, 1985; Holcomb and Goodrich, 1976).

The process of inhibiting life-long visual behaviour and replacing it with new fixating and scanning behaviour takes a considerable amount of time and effort, and it can be very tiring to the client. Plenty of encouragement and frequent breaks should be given, and successes should be praised. With extended practice, and this could involve months of continual effort, clients can be taught to recognize people by their gait, their overall outline and their posture. Hairstyles and dress are additional cues which can help a client who has difficulty in recognizing a face to identify a person at a glance.

Field defects arising from brain damage tend to form a separate category. Chapter 5 describes how a lesion in the right parietal area can cause a left-sided neglect, and this can exist in the presence of an intact field. It is important to differentiate between a neglect syndrome and a left-sided hemianopia because clients suffering from left-sided neglect are much more difficult to deal with than those who simply have a hemianopia caused by a lesion lower down in the optic tract.

PSYCHOLOGICAL FACTORS

There is another aspect of residual sight which has not been given sufficient attention, and that is the person's attitude towards it in the initial stages of adjustment to sight loss. Whereas the person who loses almost all of their sight suddenly may go into a state of shock, the person who loses only some of their sight may come to deny the amount of residual vision with which they are left. There appear to be two reasons for this. The first is that sighted people cannot understand why it is that a person with low vision may be able to walk about without bumping into things, yet be unable to read print or recognize a face at more than two paces. Conversely, they may find it incomprehensible that a person with tunnel vision may be able to read the time on the town clock, but trip on the kerb as they are doing so.

In order to avoid being labelled as a fraud, some people with residual sight fake worse than they really are, and this is perfectly understandable, given that they are neither completely blind nor fully sighted. Even people who are legitimately registered as blind, but yet possess good central vision, can feel very guilty about the apparent contradiction between the label they have been given by society and the level of their social performance, which may be predominantly visual. They cannot reconcile the fact that they are labelled blind, but that they can see. This is because of the contradiction between the social conception of blind as meaning 'without sight' and the legal definition of blind which is based on criteria such as degree of acuity and integrity of the visual field.

In an attempt to live up to the label, a person might try to 'fake bad'; that is to say, behave as if they had little or no sight at all. But faking bad often necessitates the adoption of further devious strategies, such as 'surreptitious' looking while maintaining the role stereotype of the totally blind person for the benefit of the sighted onlooker. Such play-acting, although it may reduce certain forms of social stress, exacts its price by producing internal psychological stress, as well as sapping self-esteem through guilt. By trying not to appear to be a fraud, the client ends up feeling even more of a fraud, so that such strategies are self-defeating and should be discouraged by means of open discussion about the problem.

The second reason is that people remember how the world was when their sight was all right, and to compare their current vision with such clear memories of their former vision is painful. One solution to this is to shift one's attention away from current visual input altogether, in order to escape the pain produced by the comparison with what is remembered. The net effect is the same, however: sight which could be of considerable use is ignored, at the expense of optimal functioning. If you suspect that a client has much more useful sight than they are prepared to admit, then it is worth discussing the client's own attitudes to his sight as well as asking him to try to be as honest as possible about what he can and cannot see.

Another psychological factor which many people do not fully acknowledge is that low vision involves the person in a lot of effort. Great amounts of concentration are required to extract useful information, and this is tiring. When a person gets tired they tend to process less information, either by not looking so carefully or by letting their attention wander. Clients often report that worries and anxieties interfere with how well they see on any particular day, so that a relaxed client is going to be able to perform better than one who is apprehensive or preoccupied with internal problems. If your client seems to be having an off day, make sure that he has a chance to rest his eyes and to talk over any problems which might be distracting or fatiguing him.

FUNCTIONAL ASSESSMENT

Given the foregoing considerations, it must be recognized that the category 'low vision' covers a diverse range of visual problems with no less diverse a range of solutions. There is no such thing as a 'typical' low-vision client, and that is why it is so important to carry out a full, functional assessment of visual abilities. When we talk of functional assessment, it is important to recognize that a person's ability to carry out any particular task is a joint product of their own abilities or skills, and the environment in which they are being assessed.

Rehabilitation has been seen traditionally as the training of people to behave differently in the same environment, at the expense of modifying the environment to suit their disabilities. It is important that we realize how effective we can be by concentrating as much on the environment as we do upon the individual. Indeed, many people will be able to benefit as much from careful consideration of lighting and contrast as they will from visual aids such as spectacles, magnifiers and telescopes.

A full functional assessment will therefore need to take into consideration both client and environmental factors, and the client's ability to carry out a wide variety of independent living tasks has to be assessed in a range of lighting conditions in order to ascertain the potential for his remaining a predominantly visual person (Carter, 1983). This means that you should be able to increase illumination levels by means of supplementing the client's existing lighting, and observe any changes in his performance as a result. There is no point in assessing a client in a dingy kitchen and concluding that his inability to pour water into a teapot is due to his poor sight, when increasing the illumination might make the task much easier to perform.

Similarly, when assessing independent outdoor mobility, it is important to see how well the client is able to move around at dusk and at night under artificial light. The whole point of a functional low vision assessment is to ascertain how much the client's sight can be relied upon in any lighting setting. If there is any doubt at all about how dependable a client's residual sight is in relation to any specific task, then alternative methods have to be taught in order for the client to feel confident that he can handle novel situations. Thus if he cannot judge the distance or approach rate of vehicles, he should be taught listening skills and how to make sound judgments based on them.

Although vision testing in the clinic is a relatively exact science, assessing a client's visual functioning in the home setting is a much less precise exercise. For example, acuity figures are unlikely to relate to mobility performance, and field defects may not affect reading ability. In recognition of this state of affairs, researchers are trying to develop vision screening questionnaires consisting of items which hopefully capture a range of everyday activities. One such questionnaire is the Vision Screening Questionnaire (Horowitz, Teresi and Cassels, 1991). This 15-item questionnaire has the potential of helping a rehabilitation worker assess the limits to independent living skills imposed by a visual impairment, and it can also be used to evaluate the effectiveness of any intervention carried out.

ACUITY AND LEVELS OF ILLUMINATION

In the normal eye, the image on the retina has a resolution limited only by the size of the receptor cell. In an eye which has a corneal opacity, or one in which the aqueous or vitreous fluid has become cloudy, the resolution is limited even further. The presence of any opacity which lies in the path of the light rays reaching the retina causes a loss of acuity and a lowering of contrast sensitivity. Chapter 4 explains how all visual information consists of light structured by virtue of being reflected from surfaces. In the case of any surface, we must recognize that the amount of light reaching the eye from it depends upon three distinct factors: the intensity of the light source, the distance of the light source from the surface, and the reflectance of the surface itself. Together, these factors affect what we perceive as contrast. Let us now consider how this comes about.

Contrast is important for visual control of locomotion because it is through contrast that surfaces are specified in relation to one another. Research has shown the importance of contrast sensitivity in mobility (Long, Rieser and Hill, 1990), but contrast is also important for the legibility of print (Perfetti, 1985). With suitable increases in contrast, considerable improvement in function can be achieved in many cases. An examination of this relationship between lighting levels and perceived contrast will help us to understand how the one can radically affect the other.

Contrast is defined as the ratio of reflectance of one surface to another. Reflectance is determined entirely by the nature of the surface upon which the light falls. Some surfaces reflect light considerably, and are thereby perceived as being lighter in tone to surfaces which by contrast absorb light, and thereby appear dark. But levels of illumination can affect the perceived contrast between surfaces, independently of their reflectance, which remains the same. How does this come about?

Because of the way in which the eye and the brain work, some changes in stimulation can be detected, whereas others cannot. The basic psychophysical unit of detection is known as the 'just noticeable difference', or JND. JNDs are related in a fairly regular way to aspects of the physical world such as the loudness of sounds or the brightness of illuminated surfaces. Let us imagine a purely hypothetical perceptual system which requires a difference in stimulation of eight units of light energy, whatever these units might be, in order to produce one JND. This means that any difference which is less than eight units will not be perceived at all, whereas any change above eight units will be perceived.

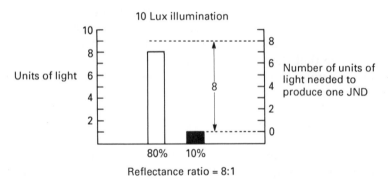

Figure 9.1 Illuminating surfaces using low-power light (10 lux).

Let us now take the basic case of two adjacent surfaces, one of which reflects a lot of light, the other of which absorbs a lot of light. Figure 9.1 illustrates the situation where a surface with a reflectance factor of 80% is located adjacent to a surface which has a reflectance factor of 10%. The reflectance ratio is therefore 8 to 1. Suppose we illuminate both of those surfaces with a light source which produces, say 10 lux (a lux is a unit of luminous flux related to the amount of energy in the light source). The first surface reflects eight units of light back to the eye, whereas the second surface reflects back one unit to the eye. This is a difference of seven units, which is just not enough to produce a JND. In order for the two surfaces to be discriminable, the difference would have to exceed the size of the dotted area.

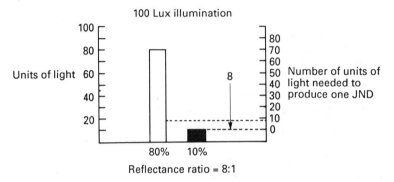

Figure 9.2 Illuminating surfaces using more powerful light (100 lux).

Now, let us illuminate the surfaces with a much more powerful light source; say, 100 lux. This is illustrated in Figure 9.2. Note that the only difference between the two figures is that the scale on the left has changed with the increase in illumination: everything else remains the same. The first surface now reflects 80 units back to the eye, whereas the second surface reflects back 10 units., This is a difference of 70 units, which is not only well above the level of detection, but enables the individual potentially to distinguish between a range of over eight additional inter/ening surface tones. So that by increasing the illumination ten fold, the client's visual perception may have been increased by a significant amount.

Although many clients can be helped to remain predominantly visual in the ways in which they go about things by the simple expedient of increasing levels of illumination, there is at least one exception to this general rule, and there are probably others. A client who has a cataract near the centre of the lens is likely to be further handicapped by increases in illumination because an increase in light level is responded to by a decrease in pupil size. The net result of this is that light rays are directed more through the centre of the lens, which is where the opacity lies. This effectively increases the scattering of light as it passes through the lens, resulting in a reduced ability to discriminate surfaces. In such cases it is best to experiment with lighting levels in order to find that which is best for the client.

Increases in illumination can be achieved quite easily and at little initial and subsequent running cost. Even relatively modest modifications of existing lighting can produce marked improvements in task performance. Research by Cullinan, Gould, Silver *et al.* (1977) showed that lighting augmented by the introduction of a reading lamp with a 60 watt bulb benefitted over 80% of clients. Not only reading, but fine tasks such as sewing require higher levels of illumination than are usually present, and tasks where safety is paramount, for example, in the kitchen, are all helped by improving lighting levels.

As well as helping to improving hand–eye co-ordination, visual control of indoor mobility is greatly assisted by a general increase in illumination. Research carried out at the Blind Mobility Research Unit has shown how physical contact with obstacles is reduced simply by increasing lighting levels, and this must contribute to safety. Falls in the elderly can be serious, resulting in fractures of the femoral head, and any improvement in lighting in the home is likely to help prevent such accidents. This can often mean the difference between living independently at home and spending the remainder of life in some form of care or sheltered accommodation.

When deciding on how much light levels need to be augmented, it is best to determine this by means of a light meter. These are available from most photographic suppliers and they need not be expensive. If you cannot obtain one which gives readings in lux, ask for a conversion chart. In addition, you will need to know how many lux per watt various sources of artificial light produce. Gas-filled tubes are more efficient than conventional tungsten filament bulbs, and miniature halogen lamps are also very efficient. Recent advances in technology have resulted in the development of gas-filled luminaires which can be plugged into an ordinary light socket via an inexpensive adaptor.

Cost is usually an important consideration, given that many clients will be reluctant to take up a suggestion which is going to increase their electricity bills, so it would be wise to visit your local lighting centre to see what new products are available. A word of warning is, however, appropriate. Manufacturers may advertise that their gas-filled luminaires are as much as five or even eight times as efficient as a tungsten equivalent of the same wattage. In practice, this is unlikely to be true. In my own experience, the light falling on a surface from such a luminaire is likely to be only around twice that obtainable from a similar wattage tungsten lamp. So be aware that manufacturers' claims, although not strictly false, are often unduly optimistic in practice, since home conditions may not produce an optimal result.

Additionally, the inverse square law, illustrated in Figure 9.3, should not be forgotten. A light moved to twice its distance from a surface produces only a *quarter* of the illumination it

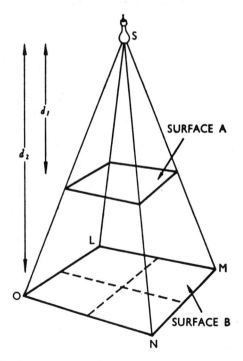

Figure 9.3 The inverse square law.

did before, not just half. This means that if your client lives in an old house with high ceilings, the general illumination is likely to be quite poor at floor level. Use your light meter to measure the brightness of the surface and then calculate how many lux the overhead lighting will need to be to produce the desired level at that distance. If ceilings are painted in a dark colour, or if they have become badly discoloured through smoking, suggest that your client consider having them painted in a brilliant white emulsion which will reflect daylight and artificial light better.

It should also be recognized that floor coverings tend to be dark in colour, absorbing huge amounts of the light falling on them. Since light-coloured floors quickly get dirty, people tend to chose dark shades for floor coverings. Try to introduce contrast at strategic points where surfaces might change their level, for example, at the top of stairs. If it is not possible to do this on the surface itself, then consider placing a conspicuous marker on the wall, or place a large and obvious object at the point in question so that it acts as a cue to a change in surface level.

In addition to having heavy curtains, some people use net drapes over their windows, which they may not draw back fully during the day. They may like the feeling of privacy that this gives, but you should point out the importance of allowing as much light as possible into rooms and, wherever possible, persuade your client to consider the advantages to be gained by doing away with such barriers to good illumination.

Outdoors, too, lighting levels should be adequate for safe mobility outside daylight hours, which can be quite short in some countries. A client who lives up a flight of stairs will need a good source of illumination on the steps, and a handrail to hold on to. However, a word of warning is appropriate here. The light should not be positioned in such a manner as to throw a sharp shadow of one step across the next one, as a client with a visual disability might easily mistake the hard edge of the shadow for the edge of the step, with disastrous consequences.

STRATEGIES DEVISED BY LOW-VISION CLIENTS

A number of years ago the Blind Mobility Research Unit was involved in a piece of research in collaboration with the Royal

National Institute for the Blind at their rehabilitation centre at Torquay. The aim of this work was to discover better ways of assessing and training clients in the use of their residual vision, and a number of useful findings emerged from this study, some of which have been reported elsewhere (Dodds and Davis, 1989). What has not been reported was how a number of handy little tips were often being passed on from one client to another, and these came out during discussion groups which were set up to encourage clients to talk about their visual problems.

The researchers were struck by the degree to which clients had spontaneously discovered little ways of overcoming problems such as glare or extended adaptation times. Some clients would automatically shade their eyes with their hand, or adopt the habit of wearing a peaked cap so that they only needed to lower their heads slightly when walking into the sun. Other clients would adopt the ploy of stopping to untie and then re-tie their shoe-laces if they entered a dimly lit building, or of pausing to roll a cigarette. This would give their eyes time to adapt before they dared to move any further, while at the same time remaining socially acceptable. Wearing photochromic sunglasses was also favoured by many, as these could be quickly removed when entering a building.

On the other hand, some clients had begun to realize that they had not devised any compensatory strategies for coping with their low vision. Many of them admitted that they walked too rapidly to be able to process visual information which it was important not to miss, such as approaching obstacles. They risked the odd incident in order to appear normal to sighted onlookers. Others again had realized that the strategy they were using to overcome one problem was creating another. A client who habitually bent his head down to see ahead of his feet reported bumping into lamp-posts and trees. In the latter case it would be appropriate to train the client in the use of a guide cane so that he could free his visual attention to look ahead.

LOW-VISION TRAINING

In spite of the fact that much is known about the effectiveness of low vision training (Barraga, 1976), it is not practised systematically or even extensively in quite a number of countries, including the United Kingdom. This state of affairs is unsatisfactory, and it often means that the rehabilitation worker finds herself having to undertake some form of low-vision training as well as assessment. In the absence of in-depth training such procedures as are at her disposal may amount to little more than giving the client encouragement to use his remaining sight more, and to adopt simple strategies for optimizing visual input, such as those described in the last section. Ideally, clients should have access to a low-vision therapist who can spend time on retraining visual behaviour, but this is not always possible.

Countries such as Sweden have comprehensive low-vision teams which include a low-vision therapist who is trained specifically to rehabilitate the client's visual behaviour after he has been prescribed a low-vision aid. In the United Kingdom, low-vision clinics are based in eye hospitals, whereas the rehabilitation specialist is traditionally based in a local authority Social Services Department. This creates an undesirable structural barrier to the delivery of low-vision services and the training of people who can understand each other's role with respect to the client. Until government departments realize that a comprehensive low-vision service is a priority requiring not just restructuring of services, but also adequate resourcing, it is unlikely that this situation will change.

Although some research has been conducted into the problems of low vision, the practical implications of the work are often not obvious, and practitioners often have to discover solutions for themselves on a trial and error basis. In the United Kingdom, the Partially Sighted Society (PSS) has a number of branches from which information about practical problems of low vision can be obtained, and it publishes a magazine known as *Oculus* on a bi-monthly basis. Any useful techniques which you feel might be worth passing on to others can be given to the PSS, which may then be published. The addresses of their various branches are listed in the Appendix.

10

The family

We saw in Chapter 1 just what the rehabilitation worker can find herself up against as far as prevailing beliefs about what blind people can and cannot do, and it is within the framework of the family that such views are often shared and acted upon. Although you may perceive yourself to be the person whose primary task it is to help your client regain his independence, if your work is to stand any chance of being effective you will need to recognize that each individual is likely to be embedded in a complex network of relationships, and that your model of what is best for your client may not correspond to that of significant others in his family circle. Part of your job may therefore be to try to modify the attitudes of members of the family which might jeopardize the final outcome of your involvement.

As a consequence of one party becoming visually impaired, existing relationships are likely to have become disrupted to a greater or lesser degree, and your arrival on the scene may threaten to disrupt them even further. If you come along and attempt to change one individual in those relationships without considering the consequences of this change for others, then you can expect resistance from other people who may wish to keep him within the confines of the existing relationship. Alternatively, a person whose previous role can no longer be fulfilled may be forced to adopt a new role. An example of such a situation is the wife who, after years of being down-trodden by her over-bearing husband, decides, now that he has lost his sight, that it is time to get her own back by domineering him and forcing him into a passive role. Your efforts to increase his independence thereby present a threat which must be opposed.

A family can be thought of as a system which has its own explicit and implicit roles, rules, tensions, and checks and balances (Burnham, 1986). The system itself is comprised of a number of sub-systems, for example, the children or the grandparents, each of which will have its own internal dynamics. Although families may superficially appear to be static systems, particularly if they have existed for a long time and each member is fulfilling the role expected of them, they in fact constitute dynamic systems whose balance can be easily upset if one or more members begins to behave in a way novel to the existing interactional style. Since sight loss immediately affects existing behaviour patterns, this introduces novelty into a stable, dynamic system, and the system can respond in a number of ways, depending upon what sort of system it is to begin with.

Although workers in the field are usually aware of the dynamics of family interaction, relatively little research has been carried out in the area of vision impairment (Dumas and Sadowski, 1984). As a consequence, existing models of family relationships have had to be used in order to try to understand the response of the family to the presence of an acquired visual impairment in one of the family members. Workers such as Leinhaas (1992) have built upon such models of family dynamics to distinguish between situational, transient family adjustment in response to low vision or blindness, such as mourning, over-protectiveness or under-involvement, and what might be termed 'family disfunction' which probably has a long-standing history (Hoffman, 1981).

Setting theory on one side, let us consider the impact on family dynamics of one of the members of the family suffering a severe loss of sight. The following two examples describe how individual members of the family cope with the changes in their lives forced upon them by visual loss. In particular, the different levels of coping displayed by each family are examined, and how this relates to the final outcome. Using a classification of functional coping taken from the field of family therapy, we shall examine strengths and weaknesses within the family system which can be identified and worked on to produce an outcome which is likely to be better than that which might have occurred without appropriate intervention.

THE SMITHS

The Smith family were not comfortably off, but Mr. Smith had had a steady job at the local engineering firm, and now that the children were in their teens his wife had recently taken a part-time job at the supermarket down the road from their home. They owned an five-year-old car, of which Mr Smith had once been particularly proud, because when they had bought it two years ago it had been the newest they had managed to afford in all of their 18 years of married life. In fact, they had been looking forward to buying a new one now that they had both been earning.

It was when he had been driving one day that Mr Smith had had a near miss in this car, and having been a safe driver all of his life, he had been shaken by the experience: all the more so, since there had been no other vehicle involved. Driving out of the sun into a dimly lit underpass he had appeared to lose control of the car, and had collided with the concrete wall of the tunnel. The front wing of the car had been badly damaged, and after talking the incident over with his wife Mr Smith had decided to go for an eye test, for the first time in his life. Fortunately, the ophthalmic optician had noticed some retinal abnormalities, and had immediately sent Mr Smith to the nearest eye department at the local hospital. The consultant had told him the bad news – retinitis pigmentosa – and had informed him that he should be prepared to face the worst in the long term.

That had been a year ago and now his sight was becoming even more reduced in terms of visual field. This meant that although Mr Smith could see his family's faces, watch television and read a book, he did not have the confidence to walk alone outdoors at night, and he had tripped on the hall stairs a couple of times. Needless to say, he had lost his job at the engineering firm because he had come to be regarded as a safety risk, and he had been more or less housebound for the past few months because he could no longer drive. As he was now registered as partially sighted, Social Services had contacted him and now the rehabilitation worker had arrived on her first visit to assess his suitability for independence training.

Although the Smiths had come over as a pleasant couple in the course of the interview, the rehabilitation worker

picked up a tension in the air which she could not quite put
her finger on. Mrs Smith seemed keen that her husband should
regain his lost mobility, but the keeness seemed to lack a certain
conviction on her behalf, although it seemed genuine enough
on Mr Smith's. The rehabilitation worker said that she would
be back next week to take Mr Smith out on his first mobility
lesson, and left with a vague impression that this was going
to be one of those problem cases. Although she could not at
this stage justify such an assumption, she nonetheless wrote
it down in her records.

The following week, she returned and rang the doorbell.
No answer. 'Strange', she thought, ringing it a second time,
'I'm sure I said Tuesday afternoon at 2 p.m.'. Just as she was
about to leave, a car drew up outside the house and Mrs Smith
got out of the driver's side, shouting to Mr Smith not to move
until she got round to let him out on the passenger side. But
Mr Smith was already opening the car door and stepping
carefully onto the pavement. 'Would you just wait!' Mrs Smith
yelled with obvious irritation. 'You're just asking for trouble
trying to do it on your own.' She caught the rehabilitation
worker's eye, and composed herself, remarking to her, 'You
see the sort of problem you're going to have!' The rehabilitation worker smiled back, 'I think I'd like to have a talk with
you both before we go any further. I don't think I've explained exactly what I'll be doing as far as your husband's mobility is concerned. Do you mind if we skip the lesson and have
a chat over a cup of tea instead?'

Once inside, the rehabilitation worker began to ask the
Smiths about their lives. As they talked, a number of things
emerged which helped to place Mrs Smith's minor outburst
into perspective. In the first place, Mr Smith had never enjoyed
working at the factory, and when he had taken medical retirement, he had been glad not having to go out early every
morning and coming home tired, dirty and smelling of cleaning
fluid. He had started doing more reading, and was thinking
of perhaps taking some educational courses, since he still had
central vision. He did not feel in the slightest that losing so
much of his sight would prevent him ever from working again;
he just knew that his engineering days were over.

Mrs Smith, on the other hand, seemed less than happy that
her husband should be thinking about getting himself educated

and maybe even re-trained. She expressed resentment that she had been tied to the house all those years when the children were growing up, and boasted about how she had passed her driving test first time round only a few months ago. She said how she hoped to get a better-paid job, and how easy it would be to become manageress at the supermarket if she could only work full-time. She also said how much she appreciated coming home to a nice warm house and a meal on the table, and how clever her husband had become in the kitchen since he had all that time on his hands now. As far as mobility was concerned, Mrs Smith said that she could take her husband out in the car.

An hour later, the rehabilitation worker thanked the Smiths for the cup of tea and the chat. She said that she was glad that each of them had been so open with her and that she was looking forward to working with them both over the next few weeks. She said that she would come back next week at the same time and take Mr Smith out for an assessment of his residual sight. She emphasized how independence training did not commit anybody to a single course of action, and how it helped a person right across the board, from doing things in the home to getting out looking for a job. Each of the Smiths appeared reassured by this, and agreed to talk things over together before next week's visit.

Back at her desk, our rehabilitation worker wrote up her notes on the Smiths.

First impressions. Mr Smith appears to be well adjusted and shows initiative and motivation. His mobility needs to be assessed in a variety of lighting conditions before training with any aid. He already shows an interest in and aptitude for cooking, and although there is a conflict about whether his rehabilitation should be balanced more in favour of independent living skills rather than mobility, any successes are to be encouraged. A client with excellent potential, were it not for the fact that as a couple the Smiths appear to have different agendas. He wants a new job; she seems to want him to be houseperson while she goes out to work.

Long-term goal. Give Mr Smith full independence training without committing anybody to one particular outcome. Expect some opposition from Mrs Smith if Mr Smith shows little interest in anything other than mobility. Make sure to use this as an opportunity to discuss any conflict of interest with both of them. See part of your role as counsellor to them both, and do not proceed with any course of action without the complete agreement of both parties. Show loyalty to Mr Smith as far as the practicalities of independence training are concerned, but do not take sides on wider issues of what to do with the new-found independence.

There are several important lessons to learn from the above events and the rehabilitation worker's appraisal of the situation. In the first place, note how the shopping incident shows that her initial suspicions had basis in fact. Second, she recognizes the cause of the tension between the couple, and the car incident is very revealing about Mrs Smith's attitude to her husband doing things for himself outside of the house. Contrast her attitude on independent outdoor mobility with that on his doing the cooking, of which she thoroughly approves! Third, observe how the rehabilitation worker shows flexibility in cancelling the lesson she had planned, and instead takes time to get to know the couple better, establishing rapport with both of them. Fourth, we see how she handles the situation in a way which does not threaten either party, and enables her to proceed with her original agenda while recognizing that much negotiation has yet to take place.

One can imagine many other scenarios, all of them dependent upon how the rehabilitation worker structures the interaction and handles the information she obtains. Not all workers would be so sensitive and intelligent, or indeed, as impartial as our rehabilitation worker. A middle-aged female, having just newly qualified as a rehabilitation worker herself in spite of her husband's opposition, might have found herself unconsciously colluding with Mrs Smith; biasing Mr Smith's training in favour of indoor work, and making less than enthusiastic noises in response to Mr Smith's desire to obtain mobility training and alternative employment. A middle-aged male, having just experienced the same problems in his own marriage when his wife decides to take up work, might identify so strongly with Mr Smith's situation that he unintentionally acts in such a way so as to court the opposition of Mrs Smith from day one. In either case, such a partisan approach is unlikely to produce a satisfactory outcome.

The case of the Smiths illustrates how individual family members may cope in different ways with the loss of role of one of them. The Smiths were each showing adaptive coping: she was finding a new independence and enjoying taking over the role as major wage-earner; he was looking forward to retraining for a more interesting occupation. But they were in conflict over the issue of who was to be considered the most appropriate one to stay at home to support the major wage-earner, or indeed, who the major wage-earner was to be and whether support was even necessary. Part of the rehabilitation worker's role was to help the Smiths work through these conflicts of goal, and to arrive at a mutually acceptable contract, and she made sure that she set aside enough time alongside her skill teaching to do this.

COPING WITHIN THE FAMILY

People who work exclusively with families have identified functional and dysfunctional ways in which they can cope with trauma. Functional coping tends to reduce the stress experienced; dysfunctional coping tends to increase it. Functional coping helps to keep the system intact by maintaining satisfaction of the members which make it up. Dysfunctional coping tends to drive the system into self-destruct because members derive little satisfaction from the situation and make each other so unhappy that one of them leaves. McCubbin and Figley (1983) identify 11 characteristics that differentiate families who cope well with stress from those who do not, and their analysis is a useful one in predicting final outcome and in dictating the amount of help required.

1. Clear acceptance that there are problems to be worked out. This means that the problem is not denied, and family members recognize that they are ultimately responsible for sorting things out.
2. Family-centred locus of problem. This means shifting the focus of the stressor away from any one member of the family and recognizing it as a challenge for the whole family.

3. Problem-solving coping. This means that effective families quickly move on from identifying who is responsible for the crisis, and begin to mobilize resources to correct the situation.
4. High tolerance. This involves making allowances for an individual family member when they are clearly in crisis, and displaying kindness, patience, understanding and co-operation.
5. Clear and direct expression of commitment and affections. Committed people are able to communicate this to each other, irrespective of whether times are difficult or not.
6. Open and effective communication. Effective family members are able to communicate effectively on a wide range of topics, and the resulting interactions are of high quality.
7. High cohesion. This involves enjoying one another's company and missing the other person in their absence. It prevents abandonment.
8. Flexible family roles. Each member of the family plays a more or less elaborate set of roles. In effective families, these roles are shared, so that when one individual cannot play a role, the other can step in.
9. Efficient use of resources. This means that effective families are able to use their own as well as outside resources with ease. They also recognize the need to reciprocate this.
10. Absence of violence. Effective families do not need to have recourse to physical violence since the individual members are able to express their needs and feelings in an open way.
11. Infrequency of substance abuse. Successful families rarely include members who are addicted to substances such as alcohol or even prescribed drugs.

In families in which coping is dysfunctional, the picture is often the very opposite of the one presented above. Such family members will often:

1. Deny or misperceive the stressor.
2. Centre the problem on one member.
3. Blame one individual for the stress.
4. Show low tolerance.

5. Lack or fail to express commitment.
6. Communicate poorly.
7. Show poor cohesion.
8. Have rigid family roles.
9. Show poor resource utilization.
10. Exhibit violent behaviour.
11. Abuse substances.

Although dysfunctional families will exhibit several of the above characteristics, it is unlikely that they will exhibit all of them at once, any more than a functional family is likely to be functional on all aspects simultaneously. Looking at the Smiths, we can see what areas might be considered to be dysfunctional. First, Mrs Smith appears to be low on tolerance, hence her outburst of irritation. Second, the couple do not appear to be able to communicate their inner wishes and plans, hence the unresolved conflict. Third, they each seem to have a rather rigid view of family roles, each believing that the ideal family consists of a major bread-winner supported by another person who stays at home. Therefore the Smiths altogether score a respectable eight out of 11 on coping resources, and this predicts a good outcome.

In the event, the Smith family proved to be very rewarding to work with. The predicted objections from Mrs Smith did occur at certain points in the rehabilitation programme, but the rehabilitation worker stuck to her resolution to use these constructively to work out underlying tensions in the family unit, and to get the couple to communicate their hopes and fears better. She was also able to help each of them to understand that they were possibly clinging to old family roles which were now no longer appropriate now that the children were teenagers and would one day leave home. As responsible parents, they had each felt that one of them should stay at home to cook and generally be available should they be needed. Now they understood that each of them could have a separate career without conflict, if they so chose. In the event, Mr Smith has enrolled for further education at evening classes, but at the time of writing is still without employment. He seems quite content to be houseperson during the day, at least for the time being. Mrs Smith's prospects of gaining full-time employment look good, and both of them seem reasonably happy with the situation.

THE BROWNS

Let us now compare the Smiths with another family, this time one which was having great difficulty in adjusting to the husband's loss of sight following a stroke. Mr Brown was in his late 60s, and was already retired when he suffered the stroke, which had left him with a weakness down the left side, a considerable loss of sight and a speech problem. His wife was similarly retired, drove the family car and was evidently quite active. They owned their semi-detached house, which was now fully paid for. Mr Brown was suffering from depression, a common consequence of stroke, and was to be found sitting slumped in a chair, tears streaming from his eyes whenever anyone spoke to him. His wife provided him with a constant supply of tissues, cups of tea and soothing words, to which he responded with even more tears.

Mr Brown had agreed to be part of our research study into adjustment, and I had arranged with him and his wife, in the presence of the Social Services worker, to visit him in order to ask him some questions. As the couple lived only five minutes away from my house, I telephoned one evening to find out if it would be convenient to call some time. Mr Brown sounded most enthusiastic, and asked if I could come round right away. Not wishing to pass up the opportunity, and sensing some hidden agenda, I immediately drove round. In retrospect, my enthusiasm could be seen as naivety, but I learned a lot about family dynamics in the ensuing visits.

When I rang the doorbell Mr Brown answered without delay and ushered me into the front room. He moved confidently and looked quite a different person from the depressed individual I had seen only the week before. He explained that his wife was out shopping, and that we could probably get through the interview before she returned. I explained that he might find many of my questions upsetting, but he told me that he did not mind. After a few minutes of questioning, I asked him one of the standard questions about whether or not he felt that life was worth living, and the tears began to flow. Once he had composed himself, I carried on, and he bore up remarkably well given his demeanour the previous week.

An hour later, his wife came home, expressing her extreme displeasure at my presence with a look that could have killed. I explained the circumstances leading to my unexpected visit, but this did little to eliminate her hostility. She disappeared into the kitchen and began busying herself noisily to our obvious distraction. After a few minutes she returned and at once accused me of knowing more about her husband than she did. I passed the remark off with a joke, but it was evident that I was no longer welcome. Mrs Brown was just about to show me the door, when Mr Brown unexpectedly interjected with the order, 'Let the man stay!', immediately bursting into tears again. I arranged to call at a more mutually convenient time, and it was agreed that I could return the following week during the day.

On my return I was astonished to find Mr Brown in as tearful a state as when I had first called. Mrs Brown insisted on answering all the questions I put to her husband, who became increasingly upset. I called off the questioning and lapsed into what I hoped would appear to be an informal chat about the events leading up to Mr Brown's stroke. I was quite unprepared for what was about to emerge, but it shed considerable light on Mr Brown's emotional state, as well as the tensions which existed between the two of them.

According to Mrs Brown, her husband had brought the stroke upon himself as a direct result of his over-enthusiasm for home improvements. He had decided to build a conservatory, and every night for three weeks he had worked until three o'clock in the morning, until he had completed it. As he had to be up for work at seven, not unnaturally he had been exhausted by the end of the project. The very next week he had suffered a stroke, so that it should have been obvious to anybody that he had provoked it as a direct result of his own stupidity. Mr Brown was by this time dissolved in tears.

Once he had managed to compose himself, Mr Brown's version of the events differed in respect of the attribution of the cause of his stroke. According to him, Mrs Brown had been nagging him for months to build a conservatory, as one of her neighbours had recently had one made, and under the pressure he had set to, trying to finish the job as soon

as possible, because he knew that his wife could not stand
the mess. He agreed that he should not have rushed the work,
and also that it had contributed to his stroke, but he perceived
that his wife was ultimately to blame because of the pressure
she had put on him. Mrs Brown was by this time looking very
angry.

On trying to establish what sort of social support they had,
a bizarre story unfolded. Mrs Brown was a member of a church
which had a prayer group. Every Sunday night, after service,
this group would be invited round to the house where they
all held hands and prayed for the return of Mr Brown's sight.
This had been going on for some weeks now, with no obvious
sign that their prayers were going to be answered. One
member of the group had even begun to hint that the reason
for this was that Mr Brown's faith was perhaps not as strong
as it might be, and he was being pressured into praying harder
himself.

Mr Brown found the prayer sessions very upsetting. Everyone felt so sorry for him that he had begun to feel sorry for
himself. Some members of the prayer group even cried openly
in front of him as they felt for his sad predicament. The
platitudes which they uttered served only to drive him deeper
into despair, and the absence of any improvement in his sight
began to suggest to him that perhaps they were right: his faith
was weak after all, and that meant that he himself was weak.
Mr Brown was completely demoralized and had unwittingly
found himself in a social support system which was damaging
him further.

On a subsequent visit to the Browns I was struck with the
fact that Mr Brown's tearfulness followed a pattern which was
not obvious on the first few visits. When his wife was present,
he was perpetually in tears; when she was out, he was quite
cheerful, and wanted to talk 'man to man' with me. During
one of these talks he confided in me that he had tried to leave
his wife many years ago when he had met someone who
seemed to love him for himself and not for all the odd jobs
which he could do. Indeed, it emerged that the only way in
which he could relate to his wife was by doing things to please
her. She would then boast about his skills to friends and
neighbours, and everyone would think what a wonderful,
loving couple they were. But the relationship had been

emotionally dead for years, and now he could no longer please her.

The Browns were a couple who had very few coping resources. In terms of McCubbin and Figley's criteria (1983) they lacked acceptance of the stressor (praying for sight to return); the problem was perceived to be Mr Brown's (individual-centred); it was also perceived to be his own fault (blame-oriented); they were not emotionally in tune (absent expression of commitment and affections); they were not sharing the experience (ineffective communication); they seemed to spend quite some time apart (low family cohesion); Mrs Brown could not accept that her husband was helpless (rigid family roles); and their social support system was damaging (inefficient resource utilization). The Browns therefore only managed to score three out of 11 on coping resources.

Unlike the Smiths, the Browns made little progress and their situation is much the same today as it was two years ago. Neither is happy, but they each put up with it. To rehabilitate the Browns would have taken the efforts of a family therapist, working closely with the rehabilitation worker. But many Social Services departments do not have the luxury of having a family therapist available in such cases. Also, being given the label 'vision impaired', the individual tends to be considered from a single perspective, and the underlying family problems are not addressed. In Mr Brown's case his depression was medicalized by the rehabilitation worker, who dismissed it as an expected consequence of stroke, rather than as a genuine response to distress produced by his relationship with his wife.

One way in which the rehabilitation worker can obtain support when dealing with such cases is by cultivating a social worker in the same department and getting to know the sorts of perspective taken by people trained in social work studies. If you feel that you are going beyond your professional role boundary then declare this to your line manager and request that a social worker visit the family in order to make her own assessment of whether more specialized help is needed or whether you are able to handle the situation with support from your team. Also, consider obtaining some training in counselling skills if you do not already possess them. These will stand you in good stead for dealing with problem cases, which tend to be a bit like irregular French verbs: there seem to be as many of them as regular ones.

In this chapter we have managed only to touch on aspects of family dynamics, but we have seen enough to make us recognize that families are complex systems. In the two real life examples, we can see how important it is to get some idea of what is going on in the background. If we regard rehabilitation simply as the providing of a number of specific independence skills to one individual, then we should not be surprised to find that our best efforts are often in vain if social factors of which we are only dimly aware conspire to undo our work behind our backs. Those of you who would like to know more about how to help families should consult Murgatroyde and Wolfe (1985).

Not all families exhibit identifiable patterns of pathology. But even the most happy and well-adjusted families can harbour unconscious wishes and fears for their loved ones. Well-meaning intentions can often result in what looks to us like over-protection, but which feels to the family to be an appropriate demonstration of affection. Although the reasons individuals will give you may vary, the effects are likely to be the same; opposition to independence training. In the case of a young, visually impaired person, the parents may not wish them to increase their independence because this is likely to broaden their experiences and present them with problems. In the case of a more elderly parent, the family may see their sight loss as the beginning of the end, and prematurely force them into a more aged role than they would otherwise adopt.

This chapter shows that in order to understand the impact of visual loss upon the family, there is a need to understand its past history and how existing roles have been disrupted. One also needs to understand how the family is currently coping, and what impact these coping strategies are having on the individual who has experienced the sight loss. One must determine what hopes and plans for the future each member of the family has, and whether these are shared or kept as hidden agendas which may later interfere with our own rehabilitation goals. Only when a clear picture of the dynamics of the family has been formed and all the options available have been discussed can a plan of action proceed which will find acceptance with all concerned.

11

Taking care of yourself

We are now almost at the end of examining a wide variety of factors which can influence the outcome of rehabilitation. We have taken a look at the number of techniques of helping your client along the road to independence. We have considered ways of assessing and evaluating his learning potential; of maintaining his motivation; of boosting his morale; and of helping him deal with the stresses associated with having to learn a wide variety of new skills in what may often be a threatening environment. All of these techniques will have helped him to persevere with many difficult tasks until they are mastered, and to have made the learning experience a rewarding one. Let us now turn our attention to how we can help ourselves stay calm, reasonably sane and well-motivated in the face of the constant barrage of impossible demands which are made on us, and the frequent absence of tangible rewards which we experience in the course of our work.

The stresses associated with working with visually impaired people should not be underestimated. Whether you are employed in a local authority or work for a charitable organization, every day you are likely to experience frustrations when you find that you are unable to help a client as much as you had hoped, or in the time available to you. Such frustrations as these are common to all jobs to a greater or lesser degree, but on top of them you have the additional stress of being constantly required to enter into the world of a person who may be seriously depressed, anxious and hopeless about the future.

BURN-OUT AND ITS CAUSES

Such a constant pressure to feel what your client is feeling while remaining detached enough to be able to help him is very wearing emotionally. Some workers may take on a client's despair to such an extent that it affects their own private lives. Some may find that the relationship with their own partner and family members becomes strained as a result of their living so close to the edge of the human condition on a daily basis while those around them are not. Many workers report feelings of exhaustion or 'burn-out' after many years of working with visually impaired people, and it is worth considering this phenomenon in some detail.

The term 'burn-out' is itself a metaphor. It conjures up a picture of something which was once very much ablaze being dead, with no possibility of revitalization. Psychologically, it covers aspects of mood such as depression, states of mind such as cynicism, and avoidant coping behaviour. Burn-out has also been seen as a contagion which can spread from one individual to another. Although the disease metaphor is misplaced, it does suggest that burn-out can be experienced by a number of people who may have to cope with the same stresses from which they cannot escape.

Burn-out is particularly prevalent in any helping profession, and the reasons for it have been identified by a number of authors such as Burnard (1991), and Maslach (1982). One is that most people who choose to work with disadvantaged people tend to be idealistic, believing that they have been chosen to help improve the human condition. Such idealism is a positive quality, and the optimism and energy which characterize it are often envied by those who are more hard-bitten by years of practical experience. Idealism is often accompanied by perfectionism, so that the highest expectations are held for every client.

However, an idealistic worker will soon find that she has to compromise what may turn out to be unrealistically high standards in the face of recurrent frustrations. In spite of her own abilities and skills, factors beyond her control may outweigh her own contribution to the client's final outcome. These factors can often be present within the organization itself, rather than within the client. For example, in the case of senior management, individuals at this level may not understand the details of her work, or how important it is to her. They may subscribe at a somewhat abstract level to the overall aims of the organization, but they are likely to be more interested in promoting its image (very important for fund-raising), or even in out-doing a rival organization than they are of ensuring a well-motivated and happy work-force.

Senior management are seldom recruited from the ranks of the grass roots of the profession, tending rather to be people who have worked in industry, such as financial wizards or quality control people, or they may be retired officers from the armed services. If you are fortunate, they will have been trained as social workers or administrators, but probably so long ago that they are by now quite out of touch with the lives of everyday folk. Some management will have been recruited via the 'blindness system' itself, their only qualifications being that they themselves are blind, intelligent and determined to get on. Whatever the background of senior management, unless they show a constant willingness to keep in touch with the real difficulties which you and your client face they can often fail to appreciate the reality of your problems.

In the case of middle management, they may themselves be experiencing their own burn-out and as a consequence have little enthusiasm for taking on board anyone else's problems. They might be sympathetic to your problems, but quite unable to help you due to policy of financial constraints placed on the organization from above or beyond. Many organizations are too small to allow the development of a proper middle management structure which could comprise people with the experience and expertise to bring various professionals together. The norm tends to be for the most senior member of staff to manage her small team in isolation from other workers and with little or no line to and from the board room where the policies are shaped. Little wonder that she may begin to ask herself if there is any point in making repeated attempts to get things done when the system itself does not permit this, or even appears to work against its own stated ends.

Another problem is that it is often difficult to provide any real evidence of the effectiveness of one's intervention. Few cases are so dramatically improved that the rehabilitation

worker can feel truly proud of her efforts. A large majority
will comprise elderly people who may possess additional
handicaps and hold low expectations of themselves which you
have failed to change. Many of them will never become truly
independent; yet that is the ultimate goal of most newly
qualified rehabilitation workers. Without some evidence of
one's effectiveness, it is easy to become disillusioned with what
one is doing. So that there is an urgent need to quantify the
effectiveness of independence training in order to remind
yourself that you are helping to produce real improvements
in the quality of people's lives, and to present management
with hard evidence to support whatever case you might wish
to make.

As well as lacking intrinsic job satisfaction, many workers
feel that they do not receive the remuneration which their
efforts merit. Some people believe that rehabilitation workers
should be paid on a par with other professionals such as social
workers, because the efforts involved take the same toll. Others
argue that because social workers take longer to train, they
therefore merit a higher salary. Training agencies have a
responsibility to gear their courses into established structures
with national recognition in order to raise levels of profes-
sionalism. As things are, the reality is that rehabilitation
workers are often regarded as second rate citizens in Social
Services Departments, so that they tend to devalue themselves
in relation to other professionals.

To add to this problem, although some workers eagerly seek
promotion to administrative levels, few actually achieve it.
Those who have a career ambition are probably better off not
working in a one-to-one with clients. But most workers have
entered the profession in order to do just that, and they become
discouraged when years of effort at the coal-face go un-
rewarded and other people who may know less about visual
impairment overtake them on the promotional ladder. Until
someone takes on board the vexed question of career structure,
increased remuneration will remain a possibility only for those
pepared to give up rehabilitation work to become administrators, or those who take the initiative and seek to obtain further
qualifications.

It must also be recognized that rehabilitation of visual
impairment is not generally perceived to constitute crisis

intervention. Large numbers of people who are losing their sight are elderly, and sight deterioration tends to be slow. As a group in society they have little power as they cannot offer their labour to the market. A newspaper may make a headline story out of the failure of a local authority to detect child sexual abuse, or to 'detect' it when it is not present (a *Catch 22* familiar to social workers), but nobody is going to make a fuss if an elderly person with a visual impairment is ignored for months. So that there is the unstated belief that what the rehabilitation worker does is not that important anyway.

Furthermore, given the constraints on what services you can deliver and the realities of a sighted world where unemployment is endemic, you may secretly believe that your client's pessimistic view of the future could well prove to be more accurate than your own optimistic one. In the face of such a realization it is difficult to put on a cheerful demeanour in order to keep up your client's morale and motivation, and it is easy to understand why some workers are unprepared to throw themselves whole-heartedly into the job after having seen many clients' hopes being raised, only to be dashed at a later date.

Finally, it has to be recognized that resources are seldom allocated on a realistic basis. Workers are seldom given guidelines on how to allocate their limited time in order that their efforts produce the maximum impact. This means that a client with little likelihood of benefitting in the long term may take up more of the rehabilitation worker's time than one who is. In the absence of research which could help establish guidelines, much of the rehabilitation worker's activities must be based upon an act of faith, and if this faith should turn out to have been misplaced, demoralization is a likely consequence for all concerned.

STAGES OF DISILLUSIONMENT

People who have studied burn-out by means of interviewing staff in the human services sector have identified at a descriptive level the various stages through which burn-out proceeds (Edelwich and Brodsky, 1980). These stages must be examined so that they can be recognized before going on to develop an understanding of the psychological mechanisms which may underlie them and ways in which rehabilitation workers can act to avert them.

The first stage in burn-out is that of initial enthusiasm, optimism and energy. Setbacks are perceived as challenges and are met with by renewed efforts. Working extra hours without pay goes without saying, and job satisfaction is high. Absenteeism is unthinkable, and people work when they are feeling less than on top of the world. Staff morale is high and everyone feels valued. Staff support each other and share one another's problems. But there is danger of becoming over-involved with clients and taking the job home, thereby sowing the seeds of lack of social support from a partner when the crunch eventually comes.

The next stage is characterized by stagnation. No-one volunteers to do extra duties without time off or additional remuneration, whereas before, goodwill could be taken for granted and people often worked extra hours simply out of satisfaction that they were helping a client. People begin to spend less time thinking about the job and more time thinking about leisure activities. Thoughts about more exciting ways of spending one's time occupy the mind and more emphasis is now placed on doing things to please oneself rather than help others.

The third stage may be characterized by universal frustration. Attempts to inject vitality into one's life have failed, and the rewards of the job are still not forthcoming. Individual members of a team may find themselves falling out over relatively trivial issues, or becoming obsessed by how someone else appears to be getting on, rather than being completely occupied with the job. People may sit back and try to take stock of the situation, hoping to identify the root cause of their malaise. They may come to realize that there is nothing that they can possibly do to change things, and at this point enter into the final stage.

This stage is characterized by apathy in the face of any problem, no matter whether it is soluble or not. Workers may go through the motions, but they are emotionally dead to their own activities which are now regarded simply as a necessary evil to pay the bills. Visits to difficult or demanding clients are delayed wherever possible and, when it is not, actual teaching is avoided. Clients may simply be taken out for a guided walk or a chat over a cup of tea rather than being expected to learn any independence skills, and they may even be used unconsciously as social support for oneself. By this stage, the worker feels literally depersonalized, and is incapable of analysing how this has come about or deciding what to do about it.

PSYCHOLOGICAL SIGNS OF BURN-OUT

Once the initial euphoria of feeling on top of a new job have passed (the honeymoon period), the first signs of burn-out may appear. These are usually rather subtle, and as a result the person showing signs of it may miss several important clues which could help them prevent its course. Most of us go through periods of feeling under strain when we perceive that the job is not giving us the rewards we have become used to. We feel irritable; under constant pressure; unappreciated by our bosses and possibly our clients; frustrated by the system. If we allow this situation to continue, we may then begin to notice how tired we are; how even the thought of taking on any little extra demand exhausts us, and we may find ourselves waking in the morning feeling quite unlike getting out of bed and driving to work through the busy morning traffic.

The next stage comes when we find ourselves coming in to work feeling unable to cope with the job. We feel under the weather a lot of the time and begin to telephone in sick. When we do go to work, we notice that we seem to be on a short fuse with our colleagues, or we may pick up subtle or not so subtle messages that we are not pulling our weight in the team. We begin to feel guilty or even a failure, and become even less inclined to place ourselves in the work environment. We may end up in the doctor's surgery with a litany of vague complaints which neither we nor he can quite put a finger on. Alternatively, we find that we are genuinely run-down and unwell, suffering from repeated colds, influenza and sore throats. We never quite manage to throw off that feeling of lethargy and the general practitioner suggests that we take a break, although he may do no more at this stage.

The sequence of events outlined may be familiar to you as a description of a time in your own professional life, or you may recognize it as it applies to another professional with whom you have to interact. However, although recognizing the onset of burn-out is important, on its own it is not sufficient for you to prevent its course. What is needed is an understanding of the psychological mechanisms underlying it and a means of addressing these in a systematic fashion so that the full-blown syndrome is never allowed to develop.

Chapters 3 and 8 examined the causes of anxiety and depression in clients and identified a number of psychological factors which have been found to be highly inter-related. Emotional states were shown to be highly dependent upon two factors: first, the ways in which we behave; second, the ways in which we think about ourselves in relation to our situation in life. These two sets of factors are not independent of one another: the ways in which we think about ourselves are shaped partly by what we do and partly by what we are trying to do. If the two coincide, then we are content; if they do not, then we become discontented. Repeated discontent leads to apathy and withdrawal, and eventually to loss of morale.

PSYCHOLOGICAL PROCESSES IN BURN-OUT

As rehabilitation workers, we recognize that much of our work involves restoring clients' morale, and we have examined a number of ways in which this can be achieved. But the same psychological processes which are operating in our clients are also operating in ourselves. Equally, and by the same mechanisms, we can become demoralized. This is because we are every bit as embedded in the human condition as our clients are. But, as we have seen, processes such as demoralization and depression can be understood, prevented and resolved. Let us now look at the burn-out syndrome through the spectacles of the psychologist to see how we can apply the same techniques to our own demoralization as we do to that of our clients.

We have seen how locus of control and attributional style are factors which affect our perceptions of whether or not we are on top of things. When pressures mount, we feel less in control and when things begin to go wrong, or simply do not work out as we planned them, we tend to attribute the source of this failure either to within ourselves or to factors beyond our control. In the face of repeated failure, the only way to preserve our self-esteem, and ultimately our morale, is to attribute failure to external factors which we are powerless to control. Thus blaming poor management is a first-line strategy among discontented workers. If management suffer from the same problem, they may blame the person immediately above. He or she, in turn, may try to place the blame with those responsible for allocating resources to their department, and so on, until everybody ends up blaming the government.

If the grass-roots workers learn that the buck is forever being passed in this way, and no-one is prepared to admit the validity of their complaint, they may realize that attributing causes of failure to external circumstances is not just a psychological mechanism for preserving self-esteem, but that it is a true perception of the situation in which they find themselves. Therefore, burn-out cannot be addressed completely if we limit ourselves only to the psychological domain. Psychologists may be able to help people to see things differently, but if the perceptions which depress them are real rather than imaginary, then it would be perverse to provide people with a set of false beliefs, irrespective of how much better they might feel as a result of entertaining them.

When we recognize the validity of our perceptions, we are placed in an impossible situation. We have to turn up day after day doing our best in the knowledge that our best is but a tiny part of a whole range of external factors which impinge on our clients. Under-staffing; the complex nature and unequal levels of provision; the apparent unfairness of legislation; conflicts between local and central policies: all of these provide the backdrop against which we operate. Although our feelings of self-efficacy may remain high in relation to the specific independence skills we are able to impart, our preceived locus of control over the whole situation is likely to move from internal to external almost as a natural progression. That this should be the case is largely due to the fact that no-one consults us when policy decision affecting the lives of our clients are taken. We feel marginalized, and rightly too.

With the phenomenon of learned helplessness, which can be thought of as the opposite of self-efficacy, people who have learnt that there is no point in acting because failure is to be expected, make no attempt to act even when success is likely. They become lethargic, apathetic and eventually depressed.

I would argue, in advance of conducting research to test the idea, that depression resulting from learned helplessness and the phenomenon of burn-out look very similar both in terms of cause and course.

When the psychological symptoms of burn-out and learned helplessness are compared, it can be seen that the same set of features is present in each: depression; loss of self-esteem; low self-efficacy; an external locus of control and an external attributional style. However, similar as they are, there is one crucial behavioural difference, which may explain why not all people who are depressed feel depersonalized, whereas people suffering from burn-out do. In the case of learned helplessness, the individual simply avoids doing anything at all: in the case of burn-out, individuals cannot avoid doing anything because they have to turn out to work. Perhaps it is the fact that burned-out people cannot totally escape from the situation which makes them feel depersonalized: the recognition that their efforts are useless, but unavoidable, that makes them go through the motions of work without their hearts being in it.

Given that the same psychological mechanisms may operate in two superficially dissimilar phenomena, how can this understanding help us to avoid burn-out? When we looked at ways of preventing helplessness and increasing our clients' self-esteem, we saw how setting specific, challenging, realistic, acceptable and measurable goals could help prevent failure, reduce stress, increase feelings of efficacy and control and improve self-esteem. Perhaps we should consider addressing burn-out in the same way to see if this problem is amenable to the same solution as the problem of depression in our clients.

One of the problems facing the newly qualified rehabilitation worker is that she usually wants to help the client solve all of his problems, and feels that when she has delivered her bit she has guaranteed his continued independence. One way in which we can avoid burn-out may be to decide just what goals we should regard as legitimate for us to pursue. If we consider that it is our primary goal to teach independent living skills, then we should stick to doing just that. If, after having done this to the best of our ability, the client for whatever reason does not continue to use these skills, then perhaps we should consider this to be someone else's problem. To take an obvious example, if a client becomes proficient at Braille but then ceases to use it after a few months because he has someone at home to read for him and type letters, then one should not feel that one has failed as a rehabilitator.

Perhaps what can make the job of a rehabilitation worker so demoralizing at times is the fact that one is also a human being and a citizen, and as such one cannot ignore what comes one's way whether one is wearing a professional hat at the time or not. Also, as a citizen one is aware of political events going on around one, and when the government introduces some scheme such as rate-capping, for example, it does not require the gifts of a clairvoyant to see what the implications are going to be within our own local authority. When perceptions of this nature arise perhaps it is better to hang up one's psychological hat and reach for one's political gun. However, since the pen is mightier than the sword, perhaps one should simply keep a sharp eye on the various parties' manifestos and exert one's democratic rights at the ballot box.

Rather than 'therap' yourself into a state of contentment, why not go on the offensive? Do not help your employer to hinder you in your job. Don't become cynical, apathetic, disillusioned, demoralized or depersonalized. Do not take sick leave every few weeks. Do not drown your sorrows to the extent that you cannot teach properly in the morning; you will have enough clients doing that as it is, and you are the one who is supposed to know all about it. As we have already seen, these are avoidant or emotion-focused coping strategies, and while they might make you feel better in the short term, they are unlikely to achieve a lasting effect as far as you or your clients are concerned.

Instead, engage in positive, problem-solving strategies (Boy and Pine, 1980). If you do not receive a satisfactory answer from your line manager, move one level up with your complaint. If you still get no satisfaction, lobby one of your councillors. If this does not produce a positive response, ring up your local newspaper or freesheet and give an interview. Get in touch with local radio and say what a disgrace it is on the air. Write to your MP telling him what you think of his government's policies if he is in the party in power, or inform your Opposition MP of the situation and ask him to place the matter as a question in The House. If he or she is on your side anyway, suggest that they draft a Private Member's Bill. Better still, try to have the issue placed on a party manifesto if it is not already there.

SHARING THE PROBLEM

Rehabilitation workers can often feel very isolated in their work, and this is particularly the case with those of you who work in a local authority where you may be the only person with such expertise in your department. In the United Kingdom, professional organizations such as the Association for the Representation of Rehabilitation Officers and Workers (ARROW) exist for a number of reasons, and one of them is to provide professional back-up and support of its members where this is unavailable from elsewhere.

ARROW also issues a news-sheet known as VIZBIZ, in which members can air their views, learn of new developments in the field, and become aware of changes in legislation which might be in the pipeline. ARROW has representatives on the Joint Committee for the Mobility of Blind and Partially Sighted People: a body which hosts delegates from the Department of Transport; London Regional Transport; Sense; the National Federation of the Blind; the Blind Mobility Research Unit; the Guide Dogs for the Blind Association, and other organizations whose activities affect the lives of visually impaired people. It has also played an active part in the setting up of a Training Board, on which it has a representative. The Training Board, which is able to co-ordinate training at the various centres, is about to be replaced by a National Council, an idea which was put forward almost two decades ago.

Another professional organization which some of you may wish to join, particularly those of you who have a teaching qualification, is the Association for the Education and Welfare of the Visually Handicapped (AEWVH). Although AEWVH membership is open to parents of visually impaired children as well as their professional teachers, like ARROW, it provides a communication channel for its members, as well as giving them the opportunity to get together to exchange grievances, gossip and useful information. Together, these organizations provide social support for people who may not be able to find it in their own locale, and there is a real possibility that the two might be able to amalgamate in order to increase their overall effectiveness in monitoring standards of training: a sore point in the United Kingdom at the moment.

Those of you in the United Kingdom who may experience frustration at being unable to access information, should consider three very useful organizations which have a fund of practical knowledge at their fingertips. One is the Partially Sighted Society, which has branches throughout the country. They have expertise on lighting, contrast and visual aids such as magnifiers and telescopes. Another is the Disabled Living Foundation whose headquarters are in London. Although they cater for a wide spectrum of disabilities they have a kitchen which is specially adapted for use by people with a visual impairment, and this can be visited by prior appointment. Both of these organizations produce information packs and lists of suppliers of specialized equipment. Finally, do not forget the BBC's *In Touch* handbook of organizations which can help visually impaired people in a variety of ways.

SUMMARY AND CONCLUSIONS

In the course of these 11 chapters we have covered a wide range of topics and perspectives, ranging from the physiological, through the psychological, to the social and the environmental. The problems associated with visual impairment and blindness can therefore be seen to penetrate every aspect of human existence, and it is now easy to understand why they hold such an intellectual fascination for us on the one hand and how, on the other, they can engage our feelings of wanting to change things for the better. But intellectual stimulation and good intentions do not of themselves produce the most effective action, and it is hoped that the material presented here will prove to be of practical use to workers with real-life problems.

Over the past few years a number of surveys into the independent living skills of blind and visually impaired people have been conducted. The results of such surveys have invariably been depressing, given the amounts of effort put in by various professionals to help their clients regain their independence. For example, the Nottingham Survey (Clark-Carter, Howarth, Heyes *et al.*, 1981) found that in spite of the introduction of the long cane in the United Kingdom some

20 years previously, levels of independent mobility had not changed significantly since before mobility training had been available (Gray and Todd, 1967).

Findings such as these have recently been echoed in other, larger-scale studies such as the RNIB's needs survey (Bruce, McKennel and Walker, 1991). Comparing levels of independent mobility of blind and visually impaired people with those of elderly sighted people (Hunt, 1978), it was found that only 64% of people aged between 16 and 59 years who had received training went out alone in the previous week, whereas 93% of the sighted aged 65 to 74 years did. Looking at those who had not received any independence training, this figure fell to as few as 45%. These findings should give us no cause for congratulation whatsoever, and we need to think long and hard about how best to target skills and resources in order to maximize the impact of rehabilitation on this problem.

Perhaps the idea of imposing help upon a person is itself a misplaced one. Maybe we should be thinking of finding ways in which people can better initiate their own requests for assistance. If the person needing help had the information as to where help could be sought and what sorts of help were available, they might be able to assert themselves better and make more effective use of resources. Personality research has shown that people of low self-esteem have their self-esteem lowered even further as a consequence of receiving help (Kobasa, 1979), and research on adjustment to sight loss (Dodds *et al.*, 1991b) has shown that low self-esteem is associated with feelings of hopelessness, a low sense of control and efficacy, low acceptance of disability and negative attitudes towards visual impairment.

Putting these two findings together suggests that imposing help gives the message that the person receiving it is in a worse state that they imagined they were, and that if the initiative for seeking genuine help is left with the individual this feeling of disempowerment may be avoided. These ideas will need to be evaluated objectively before they can be accepted, but they are already currency in social work, and techniques for empowering clients better have been developed (Mullender and Ward, 1991). The concepts lying behind these techniques may be applicable in other ways which could benefit individuals in other settings.

As a final word, it is wise to try to keep up to date with the latest ideas both in psychology and in social work. Neither profession has the monopoly over visual impairment and professional helping, and ideas from one discipline may translate quite easily into another to the mutual enhancement of each. Indeed, it is only by breaking down interdisciplinary barriers that we can hope to do justice to the complexity of clients' needs, and address them in an informed as well as a sincere way (Weber, 1991).

This will remain the challenge for the future, as the various disciplines refine their techniques and ways of defining the problem. As a rehabilitation worker, your practices should be influenced by a number of perspectives. Do not be afraid to use some of the ideas presented here in the course of your work. Try one out at a time, and see how you get on with it. Try to keep systematic records of your successes and failures and make them available to the researchers who may seldom see a blind or visually impaired person. Above all, when, in spite of all your efforts, things appear never to change for the better, accept that the struggle is the prize: without your efforts things would assuredly be worse than they are.

Appendix

The following are a few useful names and addresses of individuals or organizations.

ELECTRONIC AIDS

Sonicguide

Pulse Data International
1 Expo Place
PO Box 3044
Christchurch 6
New Zealand

Sonic Pathfinder

Dr Tony Heyes
SEETEC
Royal Guide Dogs for the Blind Association
Chandler Highway
Kew 3101
Australia

Mowat Sensor

Sensory Vision Aid
Unit 10
Cameron House
12 Castlehaven Road
London NW1 8QU

Polaron, Laser Cane and Wheelchair Pathfinder

Nurion Industries
Station Square Three
Paoli
Philadelphia 19301
USA

NOMAD

Professor Don Parkes
Institute of Behavioural Sciences
University of Newcastle
New South Wales 2308
Australia

REACT

Dr John Gill
Technical Services Department
Royal National Institute for the Blind
224 Great Portland Street
London W1A 6AA

BBC *In Touch* Handbook
British Broadcasting Support Services
PO Box 7,
London W3 6XJ

Blind Mobility Research Unit
Department of Psychology
University of Nottingham
University Park
Nottingham NG7 2D

Changing Faces
27 Cowper Street
London EC2A 4AP

Disabled Living Foundation
380–384 Harrow Road
London W9 2HU

Guide Dogs for the Blind Association
Hillfields
Burghfield Common
Reading
Berkshire RG7 3YG

Rehabilitation Department
GDBA
Chequer's Court
Station Road
Tatcham
Berkshire RG13 4ER

ROYAL NATIONAL INSTITUTE FOR THE BLIND

Head Office
224 Great Portland Street
London W1A 6AA

Employment Rehabilitation Centres:

Alwyn House
3 Wemysshall Road
Ceres
Cupar
Fife KY15 5LX

Manor House
Middle Lincombe Road
Torquay
Devon TQ1 2NG

Royal National Institute for Deaf People
105 Gower Street
London WC1E 6AH

TRAINING CENTRES FOR REHABILITATION WORKERS

National Mobility Centre
1 The Square
111 Broad Street
Edgbaston
Birmingham B15 1AF

North Regional Associaton for the Blind
Headingley Castle
Headingley Lane
Leeds LS6 2DQ

South Regional Association for the Blind
55 Eton Avenue
London NW3 3ET

PARTIALLY SIGHTED SOCIETY

Sight centres:

Dean Clarke House
Southernhay East
Exeter EX1 1PE

Grove Road
Wrexham
Clwyd LL11 1DY

Greater London Office:

62 Salisbury Road
London NW6 6RH

Sense: National Deaf–Blind and Rubella Association
311 Grays's Inn Road
London WC1 8PT

The Terence Higgins Trust
52–54 Gray's Inn Road
London WC1X 8JU

Visual Impairment Service
Scottish Sensory Centre
Moray House Institute of Education
Holyrood Road
Edinburgh EH8 8AQ

Wales Council for the Blind
Shand House
20 Newport Road
Cardiff CF2 1YB

Finally, for those of you who wish to know of the existence of any organizations in the United Kingdom which cater for the needs of blind and visually impaired people, the following may be obtained:

A Guide to UK Organizations for Visually Disabled People (1991)
Technical Research Section
Royal National Institute for the Blind
224 Great Portland Street
London W1N 6AA

The Voluntary Agencies Directory
NCVO Publications
Regent's Wharf
8 All Saints Street
London N1 9RL

References

Abramson, L.Y., Seligman, M.E.P. and Teasdale, J. (1978) Learned helplessness in humans: critique and reformulation. *Journal of Abnormal Psychology*, **87**, 49–74.

Abramson, L.Y., Metalsky, G. and Alloy, L. (1989) Hopelessness depression: a theory based sub-type of depression. *Psychological Review*, **96**, 358–72.

Armstrong, J.D. (1973) The design and production of maps for the visually handicapped. *Mobility Monograph No. 1*, University of Nottingham.

Austin, J.L. (1962) *How to do Things With Words*, Clarendon Press, Oxford.

Backman, O. and Inde, K. (1979) *Low Vision Training*, Liberhemods, Malmo, Sweden.

Bandura, A. (1977) Self-efficacy: toward a unifying theory of human behaviour. *Psychological Review*, **84**, 191–215.

Bandura, A. and Schunk, D.H. (1981) Cultivating competence, self-efficacy and intrinsic interest through proximal self-motivation. *Journal of Personality and Social Psychology*, **41**, 546–98.

Barraga, N.C. (1976) Utilization of low vision in adults who are severely visually handicapped. *New Outlook for the Blind*, **70** (5), 177–81.

Beck, A. (1989) *Cognitive Therapy and the Emotional Disorders*, Penguin, London.

Best, A.B. (1992) *Teaching Children With Visual Impairments*, Open University Press, Milton Keynes.

Blasch, B.B., Long, R.G. and Griffin-Shirley, N. (1989) Results of a national survey of electronic travel aid use. *Journal of Visual Impairment and Blindness*, **83** (9), 449–53.

Booth, T. (ed.) (1990) *Better Lives: Changing Services For People With Learning Difficulties*, Social Services Monographs: Research in Practice; Joint Unit for Social Services Research.

Booth, T., Simons, K. and Roth, W. (1990) *Outward Bound: Relocation and Community Care for People With Learning Difficulties*, Open University Press, Milton Keynes.

Bower, T.G.R. (1977) Blind babies see with their ears. *New Scientist*, **73** (1037), 255–7.

Bower, T.G.R., Broughton, J.M. and Moore, M.K. (1970) Infant responses to approaching objects: an indicator of response to distal variables. *Perception and Psychophysics*, **9**, 193–6.

Boy, A.V. and Pine, G.P. (1980) Avoiding counsellor burn-out through role renewal. *Personal and Guidance Journal*, **59**, 161–3.

Brandon, D. (1988) Snouts among the troughs. *Social Work Today*, 10 November, p. 27.

Bruce, I., McKennel, A. and Walker, E. (1991) *Survey of the needs of Blind and Visually Impaired People in England and Wales*, HMSO, London.

Burnard, P. (1991) *Coping with Stress in the Health Professions*, Chapman & Hall, London.

Burnham, J.B. (1986) *Family Therapy: First Steps Towards a Systemic Approach*, Tavistock, London.

Carter, K. (1983) Assessment of lighting, in *Understanding Low Vision* (ed. R.T. Jose), American Foundation for the Blind, New York.

Clark-Carter, D.D., Howarth, C.I., Heyes, A.D. *et al.* (1981) *The Visually Handicapped in the City of Nottingham, 1981: A Survey of their Disabilities, Mobility, Employment and Daily Living Skills*, Blind Mobility Research Unit, University of Nottingham, Nottingham.

Conyers, M. (1992) *Vision for the Future: Meeting the Challenge of Sight Loss*, Jessica Kingsley Publishers, London and Philadelphia.

Coopersmith, S. (1967) *The Antecedents of Self-Esteem*, Freedman, San Francisco.

Corey, G., Corey, M.S. and Callanan, P. (1984) *Issues and Ethics in the Helping Professions*, Brooks/Cole, Monterey, California.

Cratty, B.J. and Sams, T.A. (1968) *The Body Image of Blind Children*, American Foundation for the Blind, New York.

Cullinan, T.R., Gould, E.S., Silver, J.H. and Irvine, D. (1977) Visual disability and home lighting. *The Lancet*, **1** (Part 1), 642–4.

Cummings, R.W., Whittaker, S.G., Watson, G.R. and Budd, J.M. (1985) Scanning characters and reading with a central scotoma. *American Journal of Optometry and Physiological Optics*, **62**, 833–42.

Daugherty, W.E. (1988) Implications of acquired immunodeficiency syndrome for professionals in the field of visual impairment and blindness. *Education of the Visually Handicapped*, **20** (3),45–108.

Dickens, P. and Stallard, A. (1987) *Assessing Mentally Handicapped People: A Guide for Care Staff*, NFER-Nelson, Windsor.

Dodds, A.G. (1984) *Blind Mobility Instructors*. Seminar held at the Armitage Hall, Royal National Institute for the Blind, London.

Dodds, A.G. (1985) Mobility: blind instructors? *The New Beacon*, **LXIX** (817), 137–9.

Dodds, A.G. (1988a) *Mobility Training for Visually Handicapped People: A Person-Centred Approach*, Croom Helm, London.

Dodds, A.G. (1988b). Tactile maps and the blind user: perceptual, cognitive and behavioural factors, in *Proceedings of the Second International Symposium on Maps and Graphics for Visually Handicapped People* (eds A.F. Tatham and A.G. Dodds), King's College, London, April 20–22. Printed by the University of Nottingham.

Dodds, A.G. (1989) Motivation reconsidered: the role of self-efficacy in rehabilitation. *British Journal of Visual Impairment*, 7 (1), 11–15.

Dodds, A.G. (1991a). The psychology of rehabilitation. *British Journal of Visual Impairment* 9 (2) 38–9.

Dodds, A.G., Helawell, D.J. and Lee, M.D. (1991b) Congenitally blind children with and without retrolental fibroplasia: do they perform differently? *Journal of Visual Impairment and Blindness*, 85 (5), 225–8.

Dodds, A.G., Bailey, P., Pearson, A. and Yates, L. (1991c) Psychological factors in acquired visual impairment: the development of a scale of adjustment. *Journal of Visual Impairment and Blindness*, 85 (7), 306–10.

Dodds, A.G., Clark-Carter, D.D. and Howarth, C.I. (1984) The Sonic Pathfinder: an evaluation. *Journal of Visual Impairment and Blindness*, 78 (5), 203–6.

Dodds, A.G. and Davis, D.P. (1989) Assessment and training of low vision clients for mobility. *Journal of Visual Impairment and Blindness*, 83 (9), 439–46.

Dodds, A.G., Howarth, C.I. and Clark-Carter, D.D. (1982) The mental maps of the blind: the role of previous visual experience. *Journal of Visual Impairment and Blindness*, 78 (1) 5–12.

Dumas, A. and Sadowski, A. (1984) A family training program for adventitiously blinded and low vision veterans. *Journal of Visual Impairment and Blindness*, 78 (10), 473–8.

Edelwich, J. and Brodsky, A. (1980) *Burn-Out: Stages of Disillusionment in the Helping Professions*, Human Sciences Press, New York.

Erin, J.N. (1989) *Dimensions: Visually Impaired Persons with Multiple Disabilities*, American Federation for the Blind, New York.

Filip, S.-H., Aymanns, P. and Braukmann, W. (1986) Coping with life events: When the self comes into play, in *Self-related Cognitions in Anxiety and Motivation* (ed. R. Schwarzer), Lawrence Erlbaum Associates, Hillsdale, New Jersey.

Fiske, S.T. and Taylor, S.E. (1991) *Social Cognition*, McGraw-Hill, New York.

Freeman, P.B. and Jose, R.T. (1992) *The Art and Practice of Low Vision*, Butterworth-Heinemann, New York.

Gibson, J.J. (1966) *The Senses Considered as Perceptual Systems*, Houghton Mifflen, Boston.

Goldstein, G. and Ruthven, L. (1983) *Rehabilitation of the Brain-Injured Adult*, Plenum Press, New York and London.

Golledge, R.G. (1991) Tactual strip maps as navigational aids. *Journal of Visual Impairment and Blindness*, **85** (7), 296–301.

Gray, P.G. and Todd, J.E. (1967) *Mobility and Reading Habits of the Blind*, Government Social Survey SS 386, HMSO, London.

Haley, J. (1963) *Strategies of Psychotherapy*, Grune Stratton, New York.

Heyes, A.D. (1984) The Sonic Pathfinder: a new electronic travel aid. *Journal of Visual Impairment and Blindness*, **78** (5), 200–2.

Hill, G. and Blasch, B.B. (1980) Concept development, in *Foundations of Orientation and Mobility* (eds. R.L. Welsh and B.B. Blasch), American Foundation for the Blind, New York.

Hoffman, L. (1981) *Foundations of Family Therapy: A Conceptual Framework for Systems Change*, Basic Books, New York.

Holcomb, J.G. and Goodrich, G.L. (1976) Eccentric viewing training. *Journal of the American Optometric Assocation*, **47**, 1438–43.

Horowitz, A., Teresi, J.A. and Cassels, L.A. (1991) Development of a vision screening questionnaire for older people, in *Vision and Aging* (ed. N. Weber), The Haworth Press, New York.

Howarth, C.I. (1989) Psychotherapy: who benefits? *The Psychologist*, **2**, 149–52.

Hull, J. (1990) *Touching the Rock*, Arrow Books, London.

Humphreys, G.W. and Riddoch, M.J. (1987) *To See or Not to See*, Lawrence Earlbaum Associates, London.

Hunt, A. (1978) *The Elderly at Home: A Study of People Aged 65 and Over Living in the Community in England in 1976*, HMSO, London.

Hutchinson, J. (1991) Coping strategies: Living with visual handicap, in *Visual handicap: A Distance Learning Pack for Physiotherapists, Occupational Therapists and Other Health Care Professionals* (eds. M. Hawker and M. Davis), Disabled Living Foundation, London.

Inde, K. (1988) Why low vision rehabilitation should be given higher priorities: the complexity of the problem. *British Journal of Visual Impairment*, **6**(1), 15–17.

Isherwood, M. (1986) *Coping with Disability*, W. & R. Chambers, Edinburgh.

Jansson, G. (1985) Implications of perceptual theory for the development of non-visual aids for the visually impaired, in *Electronic Spatial Sensing for the Blind* (eds. D.H. Warren and E.R. Strelow), Riverside, California.

Jose, R.T. (1983) *Understanding Low Vision*, American Federation for the Blind, New York.

Kagan, J. (1966) Learning, attention and the issue of discovery, in *Learning by Discovery: A Critical Appraisal* (eds L.S. Shulman and E.R. Keisler), Rand McNally, Chicago.

Keislar, E.R. and Shulman, L.S. (1966) The problem of discovery: conference in retrospect, in *Learning by Discovery: A Critical*

Appraisal (eds L. S. Shulman and E.R. Keisler), Rand McNally, Chicago.

Kiester, E. (1990) *AIDS and Vision Loss*. American Foundation for the Blind/Lighthouse of San Francisco, San Francisco.

Kobasa, S.C. (1979) Stressful life events, personality and health: an inquiry into hardiness. *Journal of Personality and Social Psychology*, **37** (1), 1–11.

Lang, G., van der Molen, H., Trower, P. and Look, R. (1990) *Roles and Skills for Counsellors*, Routledge, London.

Lazarus, R.S. (1966) *Psychological Stress and the Coping Process*, McGraw-Hill, New York.

Lee, G. and Loverage, R. (1987) *The Manufacture of Disadvantage: Stigma and Social Closure*, Open University Press, Milton Keynes.

Leinhaas, M.A.M. (1992) Low vision, blindness and the complicated family. *Journal of Vision Rehabilitation*, **6** (3), 1–8.

Leonard, A.J. (1970) *The concept of minimal information required for effective mobility and suggestions for future non-visual displays*. Internal Report, Blind Mobility Research Unit, University of Nottingham.

Locke, E.A. and Latham, G.P. (1984) *Goal-Setting: A Motivational Technique that Really Works!* Prentice-Hall, Englewood Cliffs, New Jersey.

Long, R.G., Rieser, J.J. and Hill, E.W. (1990) Mobility in individuals with moderate visual impairments. *Journal of Visual Impairment and Blindness*, **84**(3), 111–18.

Luria, A.R. (1973) *The Working Brain*, Allen Lane, The Penguin Press, London.

Maslach, C. (1982) *Burnout: The Cost of Caring*, Prentice-Hall, London.

Masson, P. (1990) *Against Therapy*, Fontana, London.

McBrien, J. and Foxen, T. (1981) *Training Staff in Behavioural Methods: The EDY In-Service Course for Mental Handicap Practitioners*, Manchester University Press, Manchester.

McCubbin, H.I. and Figley, C.R. (1983) *Stress and the Family: Vol. 1. Coping with Normative Transitions*. Brunner/Mazel, New York.

Meier, M.J., Benton, A.L. and Diller, L. (1987) *Neuropsychological Rehabilitation*, Livingstone, Edinburgh.

Mettler, R. (1990) An integrated, problem-solving approach to low vision training. *Journal of Visual Impairment and Blindness*, **84** (4), 171–7.

Mikulincer, M. (1988) Reactance and helplessness following exposure to unsolved problems: the effects of attributional style. *Journal of Personality and Social Psychology*, **54** (4) 679–86.

Morgan, M.J. (1977) *Molyneux's Question: Vision, Touch and the Philosophy of Perception*, Cambridge University Press, Cambridge.

Mullender, A. and Ward, D. (1991) *Self-Directed Group Work: Users Taking Action for Empowerment*, Whiting & Birch, London.

Murgatroyd, S. and Wolfe, R. (1985) *Helping Families in Distress,* Harper & Row, London.

Oliver, M. (1990) *The Politics of Disablement,* Macmillan, London.

Paramore, J.E. and King, V.M. (1989) Ophthalmic implications of seasonal affective disorder. *Journal of the American Optometric Association,* **60**(7), 508–10.

Parkes, D. (1988) 'NOMAD': an audio-tactile tool for the acquisition, use and management of spatially distributed information by visually impaired people, in *Proceedings of the Second International Symposium on Maps and Graphics for Visually Handicapped People* (eds A.F. Tatham and A.G. Dodds), King's College, London, April 20–22. Printed by the University of Nottingham.

Partridge, J. (1990) *Changing Faces: The Challenge of Facial Disfigurement,* Penguin Books, London.

Perfetti, C.A. (1985) *Reading Ability,* Oxford University Press, New York.

Pitts, M. (1991) Rehabilitation and coping with chronic disorders, in *The Psychology of Health* (eds M. Pitts and K. Phillips), Routledge, London.

Pritchard, R.M. (1958) Visual illusions viewed as stabilised retinal images. *Quarterly Journal of Experimental Psychology,* **10**, 77–81.

Riddoch, J. (1991) Making sense of it: visual perception, in *Visual Handicap: A Distance Learning Pack for Physiotherapists, Occupational Therapists and Other Health Care Professionals* (eds M. Hawker and M. Davis) The Disabled Living Foundation, London.

Roberts, A.H. (1990) Generic adaptations to blindness: an alternative method of rehabilitation. *Journal of Visual Impairment and Blindness,* **84**(4), 151–4.

Robertson, S.E. and Brown, R.I. (1992) *Rehabilitation Counselling: Approaches in the Field of Disability,* Chapman & Hall, London.

Rock, I. and Victor, J. (1963) Vision and touch: an experimentally created conflict between the senses. *Science,* **143** 594–6.

Rosenthal, N.E., Sack, D.A., Gillin, J.C. *et al.* (1984) Seasonal affective disorder: a description of the syndrome and preliminary findings with light therapy. *Archives of General Psychiatry,* **41**, 72–80.

Rosenthal, N.E., Della Bella, P. Hahn, L. and Skewerer. R.G. (1989) Seasonal affective disorder and visual impairment: two case studies. *Journal of Clinical Psychiatry,* **50** (12), 469–72.

Rotter, J.B. (1966) Generalized expectancies for internal versus external control of reinforcement. *Psychological Monographs,* **80**, 609.

Sacks, O. (1985) *The Man Who Mistook His Wife For a Hat,* Pan Books, London.

Schein, J.D. (1986) Rehabilitating the deaf-blind client: the New Jersey plan. *Journal of Rehabilitation of the Deaf,* **19** (3–4), 5–9.

Schunk, D.H. (1984) Self-efficacy perspective on achievement behaviour. *Educational Psychologist,* **19** (1), 48–58.

Seligman, M.E.P. (1975) *Helplessness: On Depression, Development and Death*, Freedman, San Francisco.

von Senden, M. (1960) *Space and Sight*, Methuen, London.

Solberg, M.M. and Mateer, C.A. (1989) *Introduction to Cognitive Rehabilitation: Theory and Practice*, Guildford Press, New York and London.

Spencer, C., Blades M. and Morsley, K. (1989) *The Child in the Physical Environment*, John Wiley, New York.

Spielberger, C.D., Vagg, P.R., Barker, R.L. *et al.* (1980) The factor structure of the state–trait anxiety inventory, in *Stress and Anxiety* (Vol. 7) (eds I.D. Sarason and C.D. Spielberger), John Wiley, New York.

Thornton, W. (1960) *Cure for Blindness*, Hodder & Stoughton, London.

Trombly, C.A. (1983) *Occupational Therapy for Physical Dysfunction*, Williams & Wilkins, Baltimore.

Tubbs, M.E. (1986) Goal-setting: a meta-analytic examination of the empirical evidence. *Journal of Applied Psychology*, **71**, 474–83.

Tuttle, D.W. (1984) *Self-esteem and Adjusting with Blindness: The Process of Responding to Life's Demands*, Charles C. Thomas, Springfield, Illinois.

Warren, D.H. (1984) *Blindness and Early Childhood Development*, 2nd ed, American Foundation for the Blind, New York.

Weber, N. (ed.) (1991) *Vision and Aging: Issues in Social Work Practice*, Haworth Press, New York.

Weinberg, J., Diller, L., Gordon, W.A. *et al.* (1977). Visual scanning training effect on reading related tasks in acquired brain damage. *Archives of Physical Medicine and Rehabilitation*, **58**, 479–86.

Weiner, B. (1979) A theory of motivation for some classroom experiences. *Journal of Educational Psychology*, **71** 3–25.

Weiskrantz, L. (1990) *Blindsight: A Case Study and Implications*, Clarendon Press.

Wehr, T.A., Skwere, R.G., Jacobson, F.M. *et al.* (1987) Eye versus skin phototherapy of seasonal affective disorder. *Psychiatry*, **144**, 753–7.

Welsh, R.L. (1986) Psychosocial adjustment in rehabilitation. Paper presented at the Eighteenth Annual Course, The National Mobility Centre, Birmingham, UK.

Wheeler, C. (1989) *Snakewalk*, Harmony Books, New York.

WHO (1980) *International Classification of Impairments, Disabilities and Handicaps*, World Health Organisation, Geneva.

Wood, D.J., Wood, H. and Middleton, D.J. (1978) An experimental evaluation of four face-to-face teaching strategies. *International Journal of Behavioural Development*, **1**, 131–47.

Wood, R.L. and Fussey, I. (1990) *Cognitive Rehabilitation in Perspective*, Taylor & Francis, London.

Yngstrom, A. (1989) *The Tactile Map: The Surrounding World in Miniature*, paper presented at the Second International Symposium on Maps and Graphics for Visually Handicapped People, King's College, London, April 20–22.

Index

Page numbers appearing in **bold** refer to figures